Nongrowth
Planning Strategies

Earl Finkler
David L. Peterson
introduction by
William J. Toner

Published in cooperation with the
Center for Growth Alternatives

The Praeger Special Studies program—utilizing the most modern and efficient book production techniques and a selective worldwide distribution network—makes available to the academic, government, and business communities significant, timely research in U.S. and international economic, social, and political development.

Nongrowth Planning Strategies
The Developing Power of Towns, Cities, and Regions

PRAEGER SPECIAL STUDIES IN U.S. ECONOMIC, SOCIAL, AND POLITICAL ISSUES

Praeger Publishers   New York   Washington   London

Library of Congress Cataloging in Publication Data

Finkler, Earl.
    Nongrowth planning strategies.

    (Praeger special studies in U.S. economic, social,
and political issues)
    Bibliography: p.
    1. Cities and towns—Growth. 2. Cities and towns—
Planning—United States. I. Peterson, David Lee,
joint author. II. Title.
HT371.F55   309.2'62'0973   74-1730
ISBN 0-275-08310-1

PRAEGER PUBLISHERS
111 Fourth Avenue, New York, N.Y. 10003, U.S.A.
5, Cromwell Place, London SW7 2JL, England

Published in the United States of America in 1974
by Praeger Publishers, Inc.

Printed in the United States of America

The word "nongrowth" is not always appropriate to the issues discussed in this book. In many cases it would be more accurate to speak of "controlled growth," "timed growth," or "managed growth." But we elected to use "nongrowth" so as to avoid the obligation to define a new term at every turn of the text, and because the word implies a direct confrontation of the growth versus nongrowth issue.

We do not anticipate complete and instant nongrowth of population, economy, and institutions, but we are open-ended on the degree to which growth can and should be slowed down or stopped.

Most discussions of local or national growth policies are limited to questions of land use and distribution—issues like sprawl versus concentration or new towns and green belts versus ad hoc annexations and utility extensions. We attempt to go beyond these issues into a consideration of social, political, and environmental issues and a variety of other issues relevant to nongrowth, most particularly population and economic growth.

Some people believe that government should back off from explicit population policies, especially those that involve influencing the birth rate downward (although influencing the death rate through better medical care is, of course, encouraged). We don't close our minds to this issue at the local, national, or world level.

Some people believe that government has no business speaking of nongrowth and the economy in the same breath, although public sector efforts to increase the gross national product or rezone a piece of land to a more profitable classification are often applauded. We retain some options in this area.

We stress the links between population size and economic growth, noting that it is often difficult to consider one in isolation from the other. For example, recent studies in the City of Los Angeles concluded that during the period 1967-70, increases in population accounted for only about 10 percent of total increases in school cost per capita, the balance being accounted for by factors such as improved quality of service, higher wages for school employees, and the district's attempt to catch up with expenditures that had been deferred during periods of rapid growth when more immediate needs had to be met.

We also note that energy and other resource demands in the United States have generally been increasing faster than the population. At the local level, changing life styles and increased affluence can increase the demand for both lower-density living and second homes, thus exerting more pressures on land than would be estimated by a straight projection of population growth.

We are sensitive to questions of the rate of growth, the timing of growth, and the distribution of growth, but we submit that these concerns still beg the questions of absolute increments in growth related to the notions of optimal size, harmony with the natural environment, stability, and other goals.

Finally, we are emphasizing the local community and the concerned, informed citizen, but with full appreciation for the wider issues and settings and for the problems of professional planners and other experts and officials in the nongrowth area.

The manuscript for this book was basically complete at the end of 1973; new information was added through mid-1974.

More and more communities are asking whether they have to
continue to grow, how they can slow the rush, and what tools are likely
to help. At present it is difficult to achieve rational debate on the subject because there is no exact agreement on the meaning of the term
"nongrowth." The term can connote an explicit and unrestrained resistance to almost any kind of physical change in a community, be it
a new expressway, a major new shopping center, or even the destruc-
tion of a small mom and pop grocery store to make way for a super-
market. The term can also be used by those who believe that some
growth is good and some is bad but that people and cities should have
the right to make some choices.

The nongrowth movement in the United States has emerged primarily at the local level. Local communities are the laboratories for
all kinds of innovative planning and research. National growth policy
is all but nonexistent. The defeat of the proposed National Land Use
Policy Act in early 1974 illustrates the distance of the federal government from the nongrowth debate at the local level. At the same time,
the federal government makes some contribution to nongrowth attitudes
through indirect actions, such as those of the courts and the Environmental Protection Agency.

Some states, such as Hawaii, Vermont, and Oregon, have made
considerable efforts to respond to demands for growth policy. For
the most part, though, state action deals with the "outback"—rural,
recreational, and scenic areas. Growth control and management in
metropolitan regions remain the concern primarily of local agencies
of government, and secondarily, in a few instances, of regional agencies. There appears to be a very real question concerning the transferability of current state planning concepts and techniques to the
metropolitan setting. The equations that deal with physical and ecological factors would have to be substantially expanded to incorporate
the social, economic, fiscal, and governmental variables that complicate analysis in the metropolitan arena.

The subject matter of the nongrowth issue is rather poorly defined and largely unexplored in any comprehensive manner. Much
more systematic field work is needed at the local level to build upon
the emergence of nongrowth sentiment. Agencies such as the Department of Housing and Urban Development and the National Science
Foundation, which are heavily funding national comparative research
in the area of nongrowth, should be devoting equal funding and concern
to field research at the local level. Agencies such as the American

Society of Planning Officials, the National League of Cities, and the
Urban Land Institute, which claim to provide a range of services and
information to local communities, should strongly acknowledge the
legitimacy of nongrowth efforts at the local level and make a better
attempt to encourage and coordinate these efforts.

There is a real danger that nongrowth strategies may work
against the poor and racial minorities. (Of course, there is a great
deal of evidence that poor and minorities have not fared too well in
the "rapid growth" environment either.) The nongrowth debate raises
some very basic issues of equity and redistribution, and it may provide a basis for cooperative political strategies uniting environmentalists and social justice advocates in a new and more meaningful effort.
The key to responsible nongrowth, in our opinion, is some real, usually
financial, commitment to a basic redistribution of resources. This
can involve public inducements to "in-fill" abandoned central cities
before suburban or urban sprawl chews up new acreage at the fringes.
It can involve community emphasis on industrial and job development
to serve the resident unemployed and minorities, rather than attempts
to attract industries that will attract new residents or that depend on
skills not presently available in the community. It can involve quotas
or bonuses for low-income and moderate-income housing in new residential developments. Maldistribution of resources is most effectively cured by direct redistribution—the movement of hard dollars
from one set of hands to another; land use controls and planning techniques perform this function indirectly and ineffectively, even under
the best of circumstances.

Nongrowth is a new and exciting concept. The response from
established professions such as planning, law, economics, and sociology has been disappointing so far, reflecting their accumulated
stores of conventional wisdom and preconceived world views. It is
possible that the idea of nongrowth will develop into a new field in itself, expanding, altering, and perhaps even replacing "planning" as
it is now conceived, and bringing about substantial shifts in the character of the legal and economic professions. This new field of growth
analysis may prompt the development of more Renaissance men and
women who can gain some overview of the many fields it touches.

Do local communities have too much or too little freedom and
opportunity to shape their futures and control their land use patterns
in unique ways that reflect the desires and goals of local citizens?
Or are most, if not all local communities forced into the lowest common denominator—bland homogeneity, molded by the limits to local
action that are imposed by higher jurisdictions of government or by
court decisions?

Some argue that there is now too much local freedom, that local
exclusionary practices exist everywhere, limiting the opportunities

of metropolitan area residents. They point to the lack of meaningful state or regional oversight mechanisms that would require municipalities to "pay dues" for the preservation of their uniqueness—to pay some of the costs of the externalities they are thought to generate by their limitation strategies. They view the recent shift in court attitudes towards increasing turndowns of exclusionary zoning and increased attention to state overrides of local land-use power as an indication that the previous situation of too much local freedom is now being brought more into balance, more into line with regional goals and objectives.

Others argue, to the contrary, that communities seeking to preserve their uniqueness are blocked and hindered in too many and often unreasonable ways. They contend that communities should have a right to be different in size, quality of life, and other ways. They point to such cases as the recent federal district court decision in Petaluma, California, as evidence that reasonably based local efforts can be invalidated by challenges from builders. They state that the supposedly protective "environmental impact identification" requirements, while providing visibility for these impacts, do not effectively require decision makers to give any real consideration to the impacts identified.

As might be expected when speaking of national experience throughout a broad variety of jurisdictions, both arguments are partly true; in some respects and in some areas there is too much freedom to innovate, and in other respects and other areas there is too little. And while there are examples of both blatant freedom to innovate and blatant rejections of well-considered innovative strategies, the vast number of jurisdictions can be identified as somewhere in the middle. Cities sense the need to stop or control growth, to preserve some unique characteristics in the face of the creeping trend toward homogenization, but they are confused and uncertain about how far they can go in this direction and how, technically and legally, they can go about accomplishing what they would like to. They sense that real planning involves more than superficial reviews of a host of rezoning and subdivision applications, but they don't know how to slow the flow and obtain some lead time.

The phenomenon of "backlash"—court reaction to earlier, exclusionary uses of land use controls (large-lot zoning, minimum building sizes, and so forth)—complicates the debate. Court opinions invalidating these techniques are often written so broadly as to appear to limit the ability of communities to use more carefully-thought-out means of stopping growth, whether they are designed with reference to ecological carrying capacity, timing and phasing of public facilities and services, or other criteria.

And yet, despite the exclusionary zoning backlash, it seems that cities have a greater ability than they now recognize to implement land use controls through police power measures (this is the message

of The Taking Issue by Fred Bosselman and David Callies); many effective and innovative land use regulations need not be avoided merely
because of potential lawsuits from landowners who claim a loss in property value. Growth controlling restrictions, even more effective than
many of those now employed, can be supported if they are backed by
detailed evidence that they are realistic responses to specific conditions affecting the jurisdiction in question.

The key issue in the debate appears to be the criteria for applying the controls. Few communities have any detailed idea of what it
is about their local situation that is unique and deserves or requires
preservation or protection. Those few communities that are able to
state definitely what they want to preserve are likely to be more successful in having their protective regulations upheld. Thus it is no
surprise that fragile rural environments (such as the Tahoe basin) are
often the first to develop effective nongrowth strategy packages. The
same "visibility factor" seems to be at work in the few instances of
preservation of historically unique communities such as Tombstone,
Arizona and Williamsburg, Virginia. Islands such as Hawaii and
Martha's Vineyard are "daring to be different" and desert communities such as Tucson, Arizona, are thinking about doing the same.
Many people in Alaska cherish their isolation and different way of life,
and people in Boulder, Colorado, and Eugene, Oregon, appear to be
willing to pay extravagant prices to preserve unspoiled hills and mountains.

But for most cities, the issues are nowhere near as clearly drawn
as they are in the types of communities described above. The qualities
and features to be preserved in cities are more subtle and less clearly
identifiable.

It seems generally accepted that American cities and suburbs
have the "right" to develop, either rapidly or with some degree of timing and phasing, into carbon copies of one another. The unanswered
questions are, Under what circumstances can real differences be tol-
erated? What kind and degree of deviation from the norm is acceptable or desirable? We sense a growing concern among citizens of
many jurisdictions that these questions be answered. We hope that
posing our analysis from the beginning polar point of nongrowth, and
working backward to incorporate growth as the exception rather than
the rule, helps to provide the perspective shift that hastens the day
when solutions will be provided to permit diverse life styles and diverse community environments.

CONTENTS

INTRODUCTION TO
NONGROWTH ECONOMICS
William J. Toner

Does nongrowth mean economic catastrophe? In moving from nongrowth as budding philosophy to nongrowth as political strategy, it becomes apparent that this is the question over which the battle rages. It is this issue that must be our first concern.

To begin with, nongrowth strategies are usually generated in the context of a specific political unit. The political unit is usually a local government since there is no explicit national or even sub-national growth policy, since local governments are the primary "nongrowth" beneficiaries, and since local governments seem better prepared to accept their economic and social responsibilities or, at least, to move in the direction of perceived self-interest. While some form of national growth policy may evolve out of successive local and state actions, such a policy is presently as remote a possibility as clean air in Southern California. For at least the next few years, and maybe longer, the application of nongrowth strategies will take place at the local level.

While it is possible to identify local government as "the nongrowth action arena," it is far more difficult to define the dimensions of application. The application of the "nongrowth" concept appears to be based on three principal assumptions about economic growth: (1) not all local economic growth is good, (2) some types of economic growth are more beneficial than others to specific local governments, and, most important, (3) the rate, composition, and level of economic growth at the local level are matters appropriately determined by conscious, deliberate, explicit choice on the part of the local public.

In the nongrowth context, local governments may begin to question the "public welfare" returns associated with a rate, composition, and level of economic growth beyond that dictated by internal demographic requirements.* Beyond these requirements, economic growth becomes a matter of local policy choice. Local governments may then begin to pose the hard questions of who wins, who loses, and by how much. Up to this time, these questions have not been asked. They are now fundamental to the nongrowth decision-making process.

Finally, nongrowth strategies must acknowledge the demands for greater social equity that are so frequently voiced with reference

---

*Internal demographic requirements are demands placed on a community as a result of natural population growth, as opposed to those produced by in-migration.

to those high-growth areas previously identified as the exclusionary "white-flights." There is a social price to be paid for nongrowth; some have called it "environmental blackmail."* This means that local governments, electing some form of nongrowth strategy in pursuit of a continuing high quality of life, must take explicit account of the exclusionary potential of that strategy. If they do not, they are rightly doomed to failure in the courts. The message is clear: The community that wishes to pursue a nongrowth alternative must make some dollar commitments to social equity. Without such commitments the judicial life of any nongrowth strategy is in serious doubt. Social activists would do well to review this point. Nongrowth may do more to "open up the suburbs" than a host of judicial attacks on exclusionary zoning.[1]

To sum up, nongrowth actions usually involve a specific client group: local government, most frequently local governments at the urban fringe experiencing continuous pressure for urban development. Nongrowth advocates argue that not all growth is good and that some types of economic growth are more beneficial to the local community than others. They further suggest that economic growth beyond what is needed to meet internal demographic requirements is a proper matter of local policy choice. Finally, nongrowth advocates recognize the exclusionary potential of nongrowth policies and are prepared to deal with the problem through greater dollar commitment to social equity than would be made in the conventional de facto exclusionary process.

THE INSTABILITY OF RAPID GROWTH

If there is one feature that characterizes the functioning of the local economic structure under conditions of rapid growth, it is instability. Instability, the absence of economic balance, is reflected in both the private and public economic sectors. Moreover, instability is self-perpetuating, with private sector effects reverberating through an even less flexible public sector. The cycle of the construction industry is a good case in point.

Under conditions of rapid economic growth, the construction industry leads the way. In a highly competitive setting, this industry

---

*The term "environmental blackmail" was coined by a planner in, of all places, Orange County, California. The "blackmailers" would be social activists pursuing social equity programs, the black-mailees would be the local communities pursuing nongrowth for environmental purposes. The blackmail is the nongrowth strategy or program itself. The program is held hostage until it contains some positive dollar commitment to social programs.

responds to a variety of local and national pressures. Among these are (1) the local demand for housing, (2) the state of federal fiscal and especially monetary policies, (3) the weather, and (4) the cost of land. Typically, in areas of rapid growth the industry is on one long track of feast and famine. Workers in the building trades more often than not find themselves in much the same situation as migrant farm laborers. The work is seasonal but only if the crop is good.

In this setting, local areas are often characterized by "gluts" of residential, commercial, and industrial units. The construction industry often produces far more units than demand would justify. New houses stand empty, apartment vacancies skyrocket, commercial properties go begging, and local communities are left with speculative industrial white elephants. Workers prepare for several months of inactivity and the union demands increased wages because the workers never know when they will have jobs. The carpenter, plumber, or electrician who earns less than $10 an hour is uncommon. Equally uncommon is the carpenter, plumber, or electrician who works more than nine months a year.

This instability eventually extends to the public sector. These same workers now require some sort of public support: unemployment compensation, welfare, food stamps, public employment programs. In any event, the income contribution of this sector is diminished. Fewer dollars flow to the local public treasury as more dollars flow from the treasury to that same sector. The economic health of the local public sector begins to reflect that of its private clientele. This single example of the economic pitfalls of a high growth rate extends throughout the local economy. Utilities provide unused connections, the financial industry is left with loans running out, public service commitments are made, and the whole local economic structure settles to a diminished pace.

Another all-too-common phenomenon in high-growth areas is the domination of the area by a single major industry. It is an oft-heard maxim in urban economic analysis that economic diversity provides a continuing economic balance capable of absorbing national recession shocks.[2] Unfortunately, high-growth areas are prone to be dominated by single industries. Southern California, the growth mecca of the 1960s, is dominated by aerospace. With every cut in the defense aerospace budget, the Southern California economy lapses into economic shock. Seattle, another high-growth area, practically closed down with the grounding of supersonic transport (SST). Numerous cities in Florida, with their explosive tourist growth, are beginning to feel the effects of the energy shortage. Thus it appears that high-growth areas are particularly subject to economic dependency extending far beyond the local jurisdiction. These high-growth communities are vulnerable. In many instances they have created their own vulnerability. Their choice was not to choose the direction in which they would grow but to accept whatever was offered.

The public burdens stemming from this single instance of instability are aggravated by additional capital costs imposed upon the community by continued development. These capital costs—for transportation, education, recreation, and public safety, to name a few—affect the entire community. These public expenditures not only raise the immediate tax burden, they also lay the infrastructure for additional development. How often has the argument "we have gone this far so why not finish it" resulted in continuing expenditures? Beyond this, even the existing facilities and services become strained—schools become overcrowded, streets and highways congested, utility networks overburdened. Periods of high growth undermine both the capacity to deliver existing services and the ability to expand the existing capacity.[3] Little wonder, then, that local high-growth communities are not notable for their dramatic declines in property taxes but rather for enormous increases in bonded indebtedness.

Another economic characteristic of high-growth areas relates to income and housing opportunity. High-growth jurisdictions often have higher-income residents. New houses on the urban fringe share a common trait: they are expensive. Low-income citizens are not attracted to urban fringe areas by low-cost housing. Lower-income citizens might find work in some of the fringe-area industrial parks, but rarely would they find housing opportunities. The simple fact is, high-growth areas are the home of relatively wealthy escapees. They are not low-income meccas. Moreover, the additional pressures brought on a community by high growth may serve to drive existing low-income residents out. Growth, in this instance, does little if anything for the low-income population. It neither brings low-income units to the community nor serves to anchor the existing low-income population.

The economic outcome of the abdication of choice by local governments in a high-growth setting can be summarized as follows. First, the lead private actor in the development process, the construction complex, is characterized by recurring cycles of boom and bust. This cycle extends to influence a host of dependent local or regional industries. Second, high-growth areas are particularly prone to the "one-horse" economic trap;* that is, major national and international industries locating within the area are far too dependent upon outside economic factors, such as the defense budget, for their livelihood.

---

*Research on the structural and performance characteristics of urban economies under conditions of excessive growth is notably scarce.

This fact carries severe implications for the immediate and long-term economic health of the local community. Third, high-growth areas find themselves on an escalating public-cost treadmill. Increases in capital and service requirements are reflected in an increasing property tax rate or other fiscal attempts to pay the growth price. Fourth, high-growth areas provide few if any opportunities for the low-income population. At best they may provide the kind of marginal employment that was previously found in the city. Too often high-growth areas provide neither employment nor housing for the low-income population.[4] High-growth areas are the home of the wealthy; whether the wealthy are people or industries makes little difference.

The costs of excessive economic growth at the local level are best described in terms of instability. The local economic structure is too often tied to the one-horse growth trap. The public fiscal burden is weighted by increasing capital, service, and welfare costs. The population reflects an upper-income scale. As with employment, the opportunities in housing are clearly low-income restrictive. This should give cause for some reflection on the true costs and benefits of excessively high economic growth at the local level.

WINDS OF ECONOMIC CHANGE

Of all the current assumptions about growth, none is more fundamental than the assumption of its inevitability. Yet two current phenomena cast some doubt upon even this hallowed assumption: "zero population growth" (ZPG) and the "energy fix."

The pressure at the local level to meet new growth must account for the obvious economic and demographic implications of zero population growth. The historical (and sometimes hysterical) battle cry of chambers of commerce to meet new growth must now be reexamined. Growth is often viewed as inevitable when, in fact, it is not. Indeed, there is some evidence that we may be moving from ZPG to negative population growth (NPG). It may not be long before we feel the local effects of such a demographic shift. Local public facilities, especially primary schools and preschool programs, now often find themselves with excess capacity. Local industries that specialize in services to preschool children are also feeling the impact of a new shortage, a baby shortage. In time, ZPG or NPG will begin to affect demand for housing, employment, and transportation. High-growth areas with vast capital expenditures may find themselves holding a vacuous economic bag. Planning, at the local level, for excessive growth may be planning for nothing at all. If demographic projections continue their negative trend, the inevitability of growth may well go the way of the electric fork.

The current energy fix also has some clear implications for high-growth areas. Very simply, high-growth areas are energy profligate. Spreading new development based on automobile transportation wastes energy, not to mention land, air, and water. Mile after mile of new subdivision, industrial park, and shopping mall—all hallmarks of high-growth areas—are now monuments to a wasteful past. Even if the current shortage should prove a somewhat corporate creation, high-growth areas will be very much aware of their energy dependency.

The awareness of energy dependency, a certain outcome of the energy crisis, will move us further from assuming the inevitability of growth. The pattern of development is hardly inevitable. The energy fix or the memory of it will move future developments closer together. Areas of relatively greater density are energy efficient. In a recent report by Resources for the Future for New York's Regional Planning Association, the density-energy equation was made clear: "Governmental action to inhibit free-standing shopping centers, strip highway commerce, isolated offices . . . and other such elements of spread city" must be initiated. . . . We will have to go back to homes on smaller lots, substituting siting and landscaping for space; and more of our apartments will have to be clustered around commercial, office, and public facility centers."[5] It does not require a great deal of imagination to reanalyze high-growth areas in terms of energy use. In a world of energy shortage, these areas are not the economic winners. Economically, high-growth areas are in an energy fix.

While the energy requirements of high-growth areas bring into question the inevitability of any one pattern of growth, ZPG or NPG raises a forceful argument against the demographics of the assumption that growth is inevitable. But more important, it places the basic framework for nongrowth in a local economic setting.

NONGROWTH AS AN ECONOMIC FRAMEWORK

In a setting of nongrowth, local governments may assume a vastly changed posture regarding economic growth. They begin to move from a competitive stance, forever chasing any and all ratables, to a monopolistic stance, the objective of which is to exercise maximum local control over land resources.

Among other things, local governments are charged with the regulation of land use or, more broadly stated, resource allocation. Resource allocation includes the power to decide such critical economic questions as (1) whether development should be allowed to occur, (2) when development should occur, (3) where development should occur, and (4) how development should occur.

xix

Resource allocation decisions are made with the help of a variety of local policy and implementation tools ranging from simple zoning to control of utility extension, control of transportation, and negotiation with prospective developers. Local control is no fantasy. The exercise of that control, the focus of local policy choice, is what nongrowth is all about. Control of resource allocation places local governments in a dominant position to affect economic activity.

Tracing the impact of a single set of "resource allocation" decisions serves to illustrate the point. Local land use decisions determine, in large part, the quality, quantity, and distribution of housing. The quality, quantity, and distribution of housing determine, in large part, the social and economic characteristics of new residents. These characteristics of the new residents determine the "labor attractiveness" of that area for new commercial and industrial development. Thus, the reverberating influence of these initial residential land-use decisions extends to affect the structure and performance of the entire local economy. To be sure, local governments have extensive power to affect economic growth. As a result, local governments are dominant economic actors. Their decisions carry far more impact than the current urban economic wisdom seems to recognize. Nongrowth strategists merely recognize this power, elevate it to public view, and begin to legitimize it. Local governments are resource allocation monopolists.

As monopolists, local communities can exact higher prices from some prospective developers than from others, on justifiable "public interest" grounds, for the benefit of the community. For example, they can require that a new industry provide local job training programs or that a tract builder donate land for parks and schools. Cities' increasing willingness to "bargain," to exact these prices, reflects a new local economic reality. The new economic reality is simply one of choice. Previously, it was thought that all cities were merely players in a competitive game who, at one extreme, chased after growth "with all the gusto they could muster" and, at the other, were mere passive participants, absorbing whatever developments virtually anyone had to offer. In either case, they were seen as being essentially powerless.

The suggestion that local governments are far from powerless seems to fly in the face of current or, in Galbraith's terms, "conventional" urban economic wisdom.[6] Urban economists, perhaps influenced by the pervasive liberal solution of more and higher levels of government, have emphasized the dominant influence of external forces upon the economy of the city. Their techniques and analytical devices (such as expert base analysis, shift-share analysis, and input-output analysis) often uncritically assume the primary influence of external forces. No wonder, then, that cities are viewed as a mere appendage to the national economic picture.

Unfortunately, the outcome of this skewed vision carries severe negative implications, for so long as cities are perceived as merely respondents to exogenous demands it would seem foolish to consider cities as responsible for even partial solutions to their problems. With the weight of urban economic analysis resting upon the primacy of outside forces, the city is taken off the economic, environmental, and social hook. Analytic myopia, in this instance, has served to define the problems away, or at least to define away the possibility of local responsibility for solutions. The analysts argue that although problems exist the cities have no real responsibility because they have no real power. The simple fact is, the analysts are wrong.

Proponents of nongrowth suggest, with compelling evidence, that cities are far from powerless. Indeed, taken together the cities constitute a central economic force, with special interests reflecting special needs and special resource commitments. Cities control location. Cities control essential features of the public infrastructure. Cities exert fiscal power. Cities, if they choose to be, are powerful. If they so choose, local communities can be the strongest of economic actors: monopolists.

The comic book history of economics presents a depressing vision of monopolists as sneering tycoons whose factories belch black smoke over the toiling masses. While the private truth may not be all that far removed, nongrowth strategists suggest a far different role for monopolists. As monopolists, cities still function in the time-honored democratic fashion, changing only in the recognition of the power at their disposal and the exercise of that power in the interests of their constituents. Failure in either respect is recognized at the polls by the people whom the city (as government) represents. Nongrowth implies no radical constitutional shift. It does imply a vastly increased responsibility on the part of elected officials, a responsibility that arises from heretofore unrecognized powers.

Although communities have long been endowed with resource allocation monopoly power, it is only recently that the substantial dimensions of this power have been brought to public notice. Previously, this power was exercised by a tightly knit collection of local officials and dominant development interests. This is not to suggest a deep and forbidding conspiracy but rather to point out that developers, financial interests, and public officials often have tended to play mutually supportive roles. As the "benefits" of supergrowth began to overwhelm such basic community resources as air, water, land, and amenities, the key community decision points came under increasing public scrutiny. As citizens began to react at the polls, long-standing local power structures found themselves under increasing strain. Not coincidentally, this kind of situation arose in high-growth areas like San Jose, California; Ramapo, New York; and Fairfax,

Virginia. What was largely private power is now being replaced by public power. As the wrestling match continues, the public at large begins to recognize the true dimensions of this power and the responsibility it entails.

As with any enterprise, especially one as vast as the attainment of nongrowth, success cannot be guaranteed. There is no economic utopia around the nongrowth corner, but the economic cards are now, perhaps for the first time, out on the table. Unlike the unfounded previous assumption that "all growth is good," the argument for nongrowth rests on the modified assumption that "some growth is good, some growth is not good." The cities, as governments, should elect certain types of growth on the basis of identifiable need. Because they are monopolists, they have a range of choice. This is the fundamental difference which sets nongrowth apart from previous paradigms. Local governments can choose the kind of growth they want. Growth is a matter of conscious, deliberate, explicit choice.

The exercise of monopoly power by cities may take a variety of forms. For many years, elected local governments have been making economic decisions. Unfortunately, most had little idea of the choices they were making. Approving the zoning change for major aerospace development meant approving a local economic dependency that would last for 20 years and eventually result in a local rate of unemployment that all too often exceeded the national average. Approving a 500-unit apartment complex resulted in a year-long apartment glut for the entire local market and dislocations throughout that market. Local governments made and are making economic decisions. Unfortunately, these decisions are often made in a void, as if the economic consequence fell upon a single proponent. Advocates of nongrowth suggest that these decisions should occur within a far broader community context. The needs of single proponents must be seen within the framework of the larger needs of the specific community. Local governments, in a nongrowth context, make decisions in a framework of conscious, explicit policy choice.

An example may clarify this basic concept. Let us assume that a certain community has chosen a particular population-growth policy and development strategy on the basis of probable consequences for a series of community goals. The population-growth policy has been translated into a specific number of building permits per year.*

—————————

*The city of Petaluma, California, developed a similar proposal. Local builders challenged the legality of the proposal. The court ruled for the builders, finding the concept of a "quota" to be a restriction on mobility. One wonders whether making the "quota" less explicit would have made some difference. The decision is being appealed.

Further, each permit for housing is issued in a competitive process based upon developer performance in meeting several desirable criteria—for example, low-income housing, open space, or energy conservation. The city desires a certain number of units per year and a certain number of units of a particular quality to meet locally determined needs. Developers receive incentives to meet this locally determined need and also receive a form of market guarantee—that is, the dimensions of the market are well specified. The developers can have more confidence in the success of their proposed development when they know the exact number of units that will be allowed.* The market is more assured. As for the city, its needs are met as a result of explicit choice.

Some critics of nongrowth have suggested that once a community embarks upon a policy of nongrowth, its future ability to attract any economic development is severely impaired. This criticism is a refinement of the larger "nongrowth equals economic catastrophe" attack. These critics fail to account for the economic power of the particular pressured community. A community elects nongrowth in the face of external demographic and economic pressures. External demand upon the land resource of that community suggests that for some reason the community is attractive to external interests. In exercising a local option to select some developments and reject others, the community does not in any way become an economic leper in the sight of prospective developers. If anything, the higher quality of life in the community increases its attractiveness.

A variation of this criticism can be summed up in the statement, "If a community doesn't accept what it is offered, economic developments will simply go to the next town." There is a simple response to this criticism: "So what!" The criticism itself assumes that the community is attractive for a particular economic development. High-growth areas are almost invariably under enormous continuing pressure for economic development. The criticism implies that if

---

*Developers experience some difficulty in adjusting to these requirements because their perception of 'the market' is often quite removed from community need. These requirements internalize a number of costs, resulting in higher prices for their product than would normally be the case. By and large, the internalized costs are social costs. In any event, the attractiveness of such programs should not be overlooked by developers with any confidence in their ability to produce a marketable unit. Such proposals would put them in a very good market position in that for a certain community only a certain number of units will be built per unit of time. Having a guaranteed piece of the pie is a comforting position.

one development were rejected no more would be proposed! Further, it implies that in rejecting such proposals the community is rejecting a viable economic future that is somehow magically assured by whatever proposal comes down the line. It suggests that communities cannot define their own needs or opportunities. Unless one expects the entire national economy to come to a grinding halt in the very near future, the suggestion that communities must either accept development or be forever condemned to high unemployment makes little economic sense.

Each time a community accepts some economic development (or any development for that matter), it automatically rules out some aspects of future choice. Resources committed to one end cannot easily be reallocated to achieve other goals. Choosing not to commit resources to a specific development is, in a way, preserving those resources for some future use; it keeps community options open. In an age of "future shock" the attractiveness of flexibility and the ability to respond to change is an important resource in itself. The fear that "they might go elsewhere" is a poor rationale for choosing to accept developments. It ignores the future of economic development on the one hand and the desirability of community adaptability on the other.

CONCLUSION

The concept of the city as monopolist does suggest a radical change in the balance of local community power. No longer is the city the passive recipient of all growth has to offer. The city as monopolist can demand from prospective developers certain types of performance to meet certain local needs. These local needs will differ from jurisdiction to jurisdiction, as indeed they should. Developers would be required to meet these needs in return for locational guarantees from the community. Unquestionably, this increases transaction costs, but in comparison to the benefits of explicit local choice, it seems a small cost to bear.

In the past, cities have absorbed almost all externalities resulting from a characteristically automatic sequence of approval. Nongrowth strategists suggest that local communities begin to exert their monopoly powers in the larger interests of the community. The exercise of power is associated with the ability to say no as well as yes. With a policy of nongrowth, local response should reflect local need more than the interest of the single proponent. Nongrowth creates a new framework for economic choice. It is the baptism of local government as explicit economic actor whose decisions occur in a broader context of choice—choice based on the needs and desires

of its citizens first and everything else a poor second. There is
nothing in this framework conducive to economic catastrophe, just
as there is nothing in the competitive stance that guarantees economic
wealth. Nongrowth is merely a matter of consciously choosing the
kind of development that will take place. Local communities will take
more time to make such decisions, and rightly so, for their present
choices determine nothing less than their economic futures.

NOTES

1. An excellent discussion of the equity question inherent in
nongrowth is contained in an article by Michael A. Agelasto, "No-
Growth and the Poor: Equity Considerations in Controlled Growth
Policies," Planning Comment 9, nos. 1 and 2 (September 1973): 2-11.

2. For example, see Wilbur R. Thompson, A Preface to Urban
Economics (Baltimore: John Hopkins Press, 1965), especially chap.
4; Jane Jacobs, The Death and Life of Great American Cities (New
York: Vintage Books, 1961), chap. 7.

3. Werner Z. Hirsch, Urban Economic Analysis (New York:
McGraw-Hill, 1973), pp. 263-264.

4. Choose nearly any book written about urban or suburban
problems in the last five years.

5. Regional Plan Association, Inc., Resources for the Future,
Inc., "Patterns of Energy Consumption in the New York Region,"
1973 (news release), p. 2.

6. Wilbur Thompson (ibid) seems closest to accepting local
government as a principal, if not dominant, actor in the local economy.
Reference to the scant attention paid to the role of local government
is contained in Werner Z. Hirsch, op. cit., pp. 217-221, and James
Heilbrun, Urban Economic and Public Policy, (New York: St. Martin's
Press, 1974) pp. 167-169.

Nongrowth
Planning Strategies

Before moving to specific and detailed consideration of local issues and efforts, it is important that we understand the framework of concern and debate that has helped to generate and influence the discussion of the nongrowth issue at the local level. In this chapter we shall review some of the recent thinking and writing that has exposed the issue of growth at the world, national, state, and regional levels. These new viewpoints have contributed to what is now regarded as a basic "framework shift—a shift in the perspective of a growing number of persons. It is becoming increasingly clear that effective growth management policies, however defined, will require in the future combined actions on the part of decision makers at all levels.

While much of the current nongrowth action is taking place at the local level, there at least two reasons why local actors must keep continually aware of what is happening "upstairs." First, slowly moving institutional events at higher levels will help to determine the most efficient use of local resources, to define those areas where local efforts are likely to be most successful and those areas to which local resources could most profitably and productively be directed. For example, the concern of the Environmental Protection Agency (EPA) for pollution thresholds may make available measurement criteria that can be incorporated into local planning efforts. Federal concern and funding for coastal area planning can be and is being used to accelerate state and regional planning for these areas. The second reason why local actors should be aware of what is going on "upstairs" is that decisions at higher levels are usually not made in a vacuum—they can be influenced by people working from below. Perhaps the most effective local efforts are those which establish channels of communication between higher and lower levels. Such efforts establish a means by which experience gained at the local level can be most quickly brought to bear on and incorporated into regional, state, and national policy decisions.

Activities at different levels of government are, in other words, "all of a piece." Activity at each level feeds into and influences all the others. Those involved in nongrowth planning should recognize that they are responding to and helping to accelerate a general and pervasive attitude shift. As the new attitudes become increasingly prevalent, the task will shift gradually to building an institutional network that reflects them. The change will take place at all levels of government, though at differing rates of speed. The following sections outline the evolution and likely directions of nongrowth activity at the various supralocal levels of government.

INTERNATIONAL

The shift toward viewing the world as a "closed system" has taken place gradually over the past decade. History may judge that the moon shots of the 1960s did more than the writings of Adlai Stevenson, Kenneth Boulding, D. H. Meadows, and others to make people conscious of the relative size and instability of the earth and the concept of "life support systems." If the repeated presentation of these facts to the American public by all major television networks in prime time, over a long period of time, did not change attitudes, at least it created a climate of receptivity for the writings that were to follow.

Boulding's article "The Economics of the Coming Spaceship Earth," published in 1966, first outlined many of the concepts and provided the cognitive mapping and analytical frameworks for the debates of the present day.[1] The concept of a "time line" dividing the quantitative "cowboy" orientation from the qualitative "spaceman" orientation and of the gradual movement from one end of the spectrum to the other has proved to be a most useful construct, one that is applicable to the analysis of many kinds of issues and perceptions. It has made possible the measurement of "lag" and "lead" in various sectors of economic and political life, providing a useful tool for those who want to measure changes in political or other climates.

Equally important, the article points out the sharp differences between the orientations on the two sides of the line. Movement from one end of the spectrum to the other is not smooth and gradual; a great deal of shock and disorientation can be expected when the midpoint is reached. We should not have been surprised to see the fireworks that have been generated as increasing numbers of individuals and institutions approach the midpoint. (Similar examples of pain and struggle at transition points can be found throughout history, with reference to issues other than land use planning. For example, the outbursts of reaction to the first glimmerings of women's liberation

that greeted the presentations of Ibsen's Doll's House; the confusion
of audiences at some of the first performances of Stravinsky's "modern
music.")

The Club of Rome report, The Limits to Growth,[2] effectively
built upon and fleshed out Boulding's rough outline. While the findings
and conclusions of the report and its use of statistics were significant
in themselves, the reactions to the report were perhaps even more so.
The report presented detailed statistics but cautioned readers on the
tentative and illustrative use of such numerical information. Nevertheless, the traditional economic and statistical community was quick
to seize upon the numerical aspects of the presentation, raising
methodological counterarguments and data qualifications. It appears
that the objections were less to the figures themselves than to the
threat that general acceptance of the assumptions of the report might
pose to the ability of certain professions with clearly defined conventional wisdom, entry paths, and reward structures to conduct
"business and usual." The guardians of an established view of reality
can, of course, be forgiven for their tenacious defense of a system
of belief that they have found comforting and rewarding.

The initial and continuing response to the report does offer
some valuable insights about the speed with which new information
or new views can be incorporated into existing structures of thought
and belief. For example, there appears to be general disagreement
and confusion among economic analysts about the possible economic
implications of the energy shortage. It appears that few, if any, of
the sophisticated economic models developed in recent years have
incorporated detailed information on the degree to which interdependence
is likely to compound the adverse effects of energy shortage. In other
words, energy availability has usually been built into the models as
an assumption rather than treated as a significant variable. (Of course
economic analysts are not the only ones to have been caught off guard.
Planners are now scrambling to prepare ordinances that incorporate
energy conservation considerations into the planning process.)

Before proceeding to detailed discussion of the American experience at various governmental levels, it should be pointed out that
control and management of growth, in its various forms, is not in-
herently as difficult as we choose to make it. The intricacies of some
of the growth control and management schemes and strategies outlined
in the chapters to follow are often a result of our desire to balance
concern for growth control against concern for other desiderata and
to fit the entire process within constitutional constraints having to
do with private property rights.

Other nations, either more concerned about growth control or
less restricted in their ability to act, have developed more drastic
solutions, some of them repugnant to the American conscience, to be

3

sure, but many of them undoubtedly effective; they should be useful in providing us with a broader perspective. Some African and Asian cities, for example, attempt to limit migration through the use of "police permit" systems. India, Scotland, and Great Britain have absolute prohibitions on locations of employment sources in some areas; conversely, these governments give more direct encouragement to industries and provide them with incentives to locate in areas specified in national or regional growth plans.

The failures, or less than expected successes, of some major governmental growth management programs that utilized even greater powers and incentives than those now available or likely to become available in the United States lead us to anticipate the difficulties that lie ahead in the attempt to bring about a more rational set of land use patterns within the constraints of the American constitutional system.

The proposed Japanese growth redistribution program, for example, incorporates such strong national incentives as heavily funded new town programs and a "push-out tax" on industries located in the coastal areas, where expansion is not viewed as desirable. However, at the present time these incentives have been relatively ineffective in bringing about the desired dispersal of activity. Australia's growth redistribution program also seems to be foundering, and for many of the same reasons—speculation in land in areas designated by the government as potential "new city" sites (in spite of governmental attempts to enforce antispeculation measures), and a general unwillingness of the population and employer firms to redistribute themselves away from the coastal settlement concentrations.

NATIONAL

While much of the discussion at the world level has dealt with questions of growth magnitude, as one proceeds further down the geographic scale such questions come to be paralleled and often overshadowed by questions of growth distribution. In the United States, federal efforts to control absolute levels of population have been less in evidence and less successful than efforts to control distribution. It appears that the right of an individual to bear children is a more basic tenet than the right of a property owner to use his land. Federal involvement in the former area could take one of two forms: restrictions on the rate of increase in the current United States population or restrictions on immigration.

The Rockefeller report, Population Growth and the American Future,[3] outlines some of the measures that might be taken as part of an overall federal policy to regulate the rate of increase of total population. While the federal government recommends and in some cases underwrites such programs and policies in the underdeveloped world, there has been a reluctance to apply them in the United States. The findings and recommendations of the Rockefeller report have been rather generally ignored by federal policy makers. At the same time, federally supported research in such areas as infant mortality and gerontology works to raise total population levels and tends to counteract the limitation efforts described in the report. Public awareness of the findings of the report, and of the related activities of such groups as Zero Population Growth (ZPG), has had the effect of reducing the rate of live births, although it is too early to tell whether this can be regarded as a short-term or a long-term trend.

In the area of in-migration, the issues of population growth control are more shadowy and call for a different set of solutions. Certain areas of the country are affected more than others by in-migration of foreign nationals. Hawaii and California appear to be the most heavily affected states at the present time, largely by increasing Asian in-migration,and, in the case of southern California and the southwestern border states, by in-migration from adjacent Mexico.

In both these cases, added population often means added problems, since the in-migrants have far greater employment, social, health, and education problems than the resident population. In southern California, for example, many of the Mexican immigrants are families and individuals from rural Mexico who have worked their way to the growing Mexican border cities and for whom even the lowest wages in southern California are a large increase over the wages in Mexico (one hour's Los Angeles wage is approximately equivalent to one day's Mexican wage). Many Mexican in-migrants work in California to support families who remain in Mexico.

Since immigration creates problems in only a few states, it is not likely that changes in overall national policy will be instituted in response to them. In at least a few jurisdictions, however, there appears to be a need either for closer regulation of admission procedures or for compensatory payments to jurisdictions most affected by the problem population.

In the border states the problem is compounded by the fact that much of the in-migration takes place illegally. Federal border-crossing surveillance, though continually expanded, seems to be insufficient to stem the tide. Support of state and local efforts is seldom more successful. As a result, large centers such as Los Angeles, El Paso, and San Diego are doubly affected and incur extra maintenance and servicing costs, which are likely to be quite high on a per capita basis.

Debates at the federal level have traditionally addressed the distribution issues, though seldom with very much success (the many rural Congressmen are no doubt a stimulant to this kind of thinking). The experience of the Economic Development Administration in the 1960s, in its attempts both to preserve and strengthen rural America, offers a recent example of the nature of the federal effort and of the strong forces that operate to prevent immediate implementation of any meaningful population distribution policies at the national level.

Similarly, the new communities program of the Department of Housing and Urban Development (HUD) has been stalled by a lack of adequate funding in its attempt to bring about more rational population distribution patterns. This funding limitation, viewed in the perspective of the power and pervasiveness of the forces that shape the present development pattern, make it likely that most federally assisted new communities will be (as they have been to date) "satellite new towns" in existing metropolitan areas.

Thus, while reports and studies (approximately one each year) point out that nearly 100 new cities (or the population equivalent thereof) will have to be built in the next 30 years, we continue to build them, through a process of additive accretion, adjacent to and between existing concentrations rather than in independent, dispersed settings. Buildings are abandoned in the centers of the older cities and in the rural areas of the nation, while suburbia and exurbia develop apace. Periodic federal attempts to develop a national growth policy that deals with distribution problems generally conclude that the optimal growth policy provides a little something for everybody, but not sufficient change in the underlying development process to really make a significant difference.

Recent federal legislation, in the form of the "Jackson bill" (the Land Use Policy and Planning Assistance Act) promises at least an incremental beginning of a reorientation of this traditional "hands off policy" on the part of the federal government. The legislation derived more from the upward pressures from local, regional, and state governments for rational land use planning than from any conscious or continued federal concern in this direction. The proposed legislation would have allocated approximately $1 billion over eight years, primarily for assistance to state planning efforts.

At the time of this writing, in the summer of 1974, the bill, which had passed the Senate, was defeated in the House. Many of its more meaningful provisions had, been removed. Passage of the watered-down bill, would thus be primarily a symbolic victory.

As those who have followed the development of the interstate highway system and its effects on urbanization patterns can attest, land use planning decisions at the federal level are not always made where one would expect them to be made. This is so today, as the greatest federal influence on local land use planning appears in such indirect forms as Environmental Protection Agency regulations (complex source regulations, nondegradation provisions), Defense Department contract expenditures, and General Services Administration facility location decisions.

Local jurisdictions should not be criticized too harshly for attempting to act on their own, faced as they are with an uncoordinated series of federal decisions, investments, and regulations of uncertain enforceability, which add up to a somewhat random federal "nonpolicy" on stimulation and distribution of growth. While it is well for local governments to be aware of federal impacts on local planning, it would be hazardous for them to assume that the federal influence can be regarded as part of an answer to questions of local policy.

STATE

Growth management efforts at the state level are coming increasingly into prominence. As noted above, accelerating state activity was one of the major stimuli leading to national interest in the Jackson bill. Some of these state programs are documented in detail in Bosselman and Callies' The Quiet Revolution in Land Use Controls.[4] Since the publication of this volume the number of states with active land use management programs has at least doubled and the activities of those states whose programs were described have deepened. The question is no longer whether states should become involved in the growth management process but rather how they should become involved.

While in some cases, most notably Hawaii, state action sprang from a previous history of state dominance over local government in the land use planning process, in many others (Colorado, California, New York, Idaho) state involvement has come about as the result of and in response to the weakness demonstrated by certain local governments and their inability to respond to growing development pressures.

In most cases, state involvement has taken place on a selective basis; the states tend to apply their override powers and controls only to those areas and situations in which local breakdown of power and need for firmer control were most evident. Examples include:

- Massachusetts: Antisnob zoning provisions; state override to ensure distribution of low-income and moderate-income housing
- Idaho: State technical assistance to help local jurisdictions cope with adverse environmental impacts of second-home development in rural areas

7

- California: Coastline initiative
- Colorado: Legislation largely in response to the over-powering of local attempts at control by rampant development in western-slope recreation areas
- New York: The pressure of Adirondack Mountain development confronted by small jurisdictions that lacked interest or ability to control the overall (regional and statewide) impacts of development

The shift from local to statewide controls has not been easy or rapid, and where it has been achieved it has not always been as effective as some of its proponents might have hoped. In California, coastline legislation was passed by citizen initiative after repeated failure of the legislature to enact protective measures. The Colorado legislation has trod gently, dealing primarily with planning powers and provision of technical assistance, and is felt by some to have been rather ineffective in bringing about a slowdown in development of second homes in the mountain areas of the state. Even the New York State Urban Development Corporation (UDC), which held perhaps the greatest powers of any state agency in this field, has recently seen its powers to override local decisions cut back significantly. The Coastal Commission in California, like UDC in New York, has only a temporary existence. It is now engaged in dual activity—permit granting on an interim basis unitl a final coastline plan is developed in 1976 and preparation of plans for eventual submission to the legislature at that time. Limited funding and the heavy work load involved in granting permits combine to slow the Coastal Commission's efforts at planning. Pessimistic observers feel that given these constraints the best the commission can hope to do is to keep the coastal issue visible for a four-year holding period and use that time to build public sentiment for effective legislative action. The commission is one of the many state agencies that are now operating under conditions of somewhat suspended animation and are working actively to secure passage of federal legislation and funding (such as the Jackson bill) in the attempt to get sufficient money to plan more effectively during their limited lifespans.

State agencies have in most cases been careful to build in controls ensuring some local participation in the decision-making process. The California Coastal Commission operates through a series of six regional commissions, which cover the counties that border the coast. Representation on these regional commissions and on the state commission itself is delicately structured to include state and local governmental representatives as well as citizen members. Similarly, under the New York Adirondack Park Act decisions are categorized by type, with varying degrees of local and state responsibility, according to the local or regional impact of the decision in question.

In most cases the use of state powers in the land use area has been precipitated by problems of development in outlying, rural areas. These problems have been the most and the earliest visible; in some cases they are quite embarrassing to the reputation of the state, as they receive national or regional publicity. There has not yet been much state involvement in the planning of major metropolitan areas, and we can expect it to be longer in coming. State legislation dealing with rural areas has come about as a response to the activities of the increasingly powerful interstate mail order subdividers and lot sales corporations, which rose to prominence in the 1960s.

The rural development problems that require state action generally involve weak local units of government facing overwhelming development pressures. Resources of regional or statewide significance are often at stake, and the protection of such resources is usually the visible issue. There is, however, a latent issue not far below the surface in many states; it involves the potential population growth that might occur if all the lots now subdivided and sold were ever occupied. At present, only 2 to 3 percent of all lots sold in rural (desert and mountain) areas are ever occupied. It is estimated that in some states perhaps only as many as 50 percent of all lots sold are even potentially occupiable. Nevertheless, the prospect of shifts in interregional migration patterns, leading to increased occupancy of these outlying lots and the consequent demand for services on them poses a "shadow problem" of increasing concern to a number of states.

States have been far less eager to involve themselves in issues of population growth and distribution in larger, more urban metropolitan areas. This is first of all because local jurisdictions in metropolitan areas fight more tenaciously for the right to control their own development, and secondly because the inequities and problems resulting from maldistribution are less visible and less well documented in these areas. These intrametropolitan disparities appear only in cases of clear municipal breakdown (as in Newark, New Jersey, (for example) or in the form of problems affecting one functional area (most recently, in the area of schools and school finance). Recent experience suggests that state courts are more likely than state legislatures to bring about further metropolitanization of school finance. Pending suits involving such metropolitan areas as Detroit and Richmond could have a more pervasive impact on the structure of metropolitan fiscal relationships than the actions of most state legislatures. Although school budgets are but one of a number of municipal service budgets, in most metropolitan settings they comprise a relatively high proportion of dollar total of municipal service expenses—in many California cities they often make up as much as 50 percent of the total tax rate.

9

State governments, of course, have the power to change the distribution formulas for funds collected at the state level and redistributed to localities, but they seldom choose to do so. This is unfortunate, since many local land-use policies, are developed with a close eye on potential generation of ratables, often with more concern for the fiscal needs of the municipality than for the human or social needs of local or regional residents. The Minnesota "tax pooling" schemes represent one of the possibilities for state-level rationalization of the counterproductive fiscal patterns that are currently operative in most metropolitan areas.[5]

A number of states formed housing finance agencies during the 1960s. Many of these have been active in metropolitan areas. However, many if not most of these agencies were heavily dependent on a continuing flow of federally subsidized units. Some provided supplementary funding for development of such projects and developed locational standards designed to disperse the subsidized units throughout metropolitan areas in an equitable manner. Since suspension of the federal programs, the activity levels of these state agencies have dropped precipitously except in those few instances where continuing or expanded state funding has been available.

Finally, state laws governing permissible actions of municipalities can have a significant influence on the effectiveness of local growth control activity. Many states have restrictions that severely limit the cities' ability to act in such areas as annexation, prezoning, or preplanning powers. Changes in state enabling legislation dealing with local planning powers could turn out to be a far more potent form of state action than the "state programs" developed to date.

REGIONAL

It is unfortunate that in the nation's existing metropolitan regions, where most of the growth control and growth management debates are taking place and where issues of population distribution are most clearly posed (and perhaps most potentially solvable), the institutions of regional government, which might be expected to take the lead in development of strategies and policies, are weak and can seldom take an effective leadership role.

These regional councils of governments (COGs) are relative newcomers on the American governmental scene. In most cases they were formed despite the resistance of (and sometimes without full participation of) local governments. They have generally been formed at the urging or insistence of the federal government rather than as a spontaneous combined local response to a felt need for greater regional cooperation. The power of a given COG is dependent on its ability to identify and adequately review development proposals of regional significance (involving questions of staff, budget, and information availability), the dependence of the region on federal investment in support infrastructure, and the willingness of the federal government and its constituent agencies to honor the COG's suggestions with regard to approval or denial of specific projects, as expressed in the agency's "A-95" review power.

Regional councils also vary in their effectiveness, depending on the degree to which they are used as planning and policy arms by the state government. In California, for example, COGs are designated as review agencies for projects of statewide significance and for state-funded projects as well as for federally related projects. Texas COGs are used by the state government as "planning regions" for multiple purposes over and above the normal COG role.

Similarly, the potential influence of the COG is increased where its traditional function is augmented by regional responsibility for region-forming investments other than those which are state funded or federally funded. For example, the Metropolitan Council in the Minnesota Twin Cities has responsibility for metropolitan sewer planning. Its operations are supported in part by sewer service fees. Thus this expansion of responsibility brings both added control powers and added funding sources.

The degree of federal involvement in a given function can and has influenced the role of the COG. In the field of housing, for example, COGs in such areas as Dayton, Ohio; metropolitan Washington, D.C.; and metropolitan San Diego stood ready to take significant roles in equitable regional allocations of HUD-subsidized housing units. With the demise of the federal housing programs, the potential for this type of activity has been dramatically curtailed. Similar examples, such as water and sewer funding and open space funding, could be cited with reference to other federal categorical grant programs. The prospect of growing local control over federal expenditures (under general revenue sharing and the Better Communities Act) suggests that either the role of COGs, as reviewers of region-impacting investments and decisions, may decline or, alternatively, that different mechanisms will be devised to permit this function to continue in an effective manner.

Finally, even the most powerful and sophisticated COGs do not control all, or perhaps even a significant proportion, of the total federal expenditures that influence regional growth. Neither the Association of Bay Area Governments in the San Francisco Bay region nor the Comprehensive Planning Organization in San Diego County, for example, had the opportunity to comment on the impact of major shifts in Naval presence and population from northern to southern California—federal decisions that may do more to influence growth patterns in both areas than the smaller, directly development-related decisions that fall within the purview of the two COGs. Similarly, the council of governments in metropolitan Los Angeles (SCAG) is neither authorized nor equipped to review and comment on the impacts of the continuing flow of federal aerospace, defense, and other contract development dollars into the region, although these investments create development forces that have a great deal to do with the shaping and growth of that particular region.

The lack of control over federal investment is perhaps most clearly illustrated in the case of metropolitan Washington, D.C., one of the more rapidly growing Standard Metropolitan Statistical Areas (SMSA) in the nation. The local and state agencies in the metropolitan area have only limited control over the economic forces that shape much of their future, since some of the most powerful of these forces are federal decisions having to do both with the total size of the federal employee complement in the immediate Washington area and with the distribution of these employees throughout the region. Suburban Virginia and Maryland were opened up for development in the 1950s and 1960s as the result of federal decisions to disperse employees then located in the District of Columbia as a safety precaution against possible nuclear attack of the capital city. These federal relocations (which are continuing to the present day) in combination with the development of freeway access have created a series of development pressures and waves that continue to roll out over the rural areas of adjacent Maryland and Virginia.

Many analysts argue that growth management strategies require some form of regional overview. They believe that the regional perspective is necessary, since local nongrowth strategies within a region may lead to regional development patterns that are inefficient and counterproductive to the objectives of the residents of the region as a whole. In most metropolitan regions, incorporated cities have commonly been the first to apply nongrowth policies within their own boundaries. The combined result of these local policies has been to increase pressure for development in either adjacent unincorporated areas or in cities that are more receptive to development. The result is often a warping of development pressures within the region and a redirection rather than a reduction of these pressures at the regional level. Thus, sprawl development cannot be controlled or prevented unless some entity at the regional level has control over the rate of facility and service extension or is responsible for monitoring the impact of spread development.

When COGs have been effective in influencing or helping to manage growth, it has been by giving visibility to the regional nature of development issues and by gradually building, with this information, a regional consciousness of the connectedness of one action to another.

With only a few exceptions, however, COGs have been more concerned with distribution issues than with "magnitude" issues. With the recognition of the need for regional responsibility came a realization of the limits of regional government as a solution mechanism for growth planning. The suggestion that responsibility for growth policy be raised to the metropolitan or COG level may be appropriate only to the larger metropolitan areas, those where the process of governmental diffusion and fragmentation has proceeded to the greatest degree. The "regional government solution," for example, may be inappropriate for those smaller cities, particularly the independent free-standing cities and counties, where the creation of additional layers of government would complicate rather than simplify the situation. However, the existence of a metropolitan agency with A-95 or similar review powers is an asset even in the more simple governmental settings. In the Boise, Idaho region, for example, city and county governments have relied on the COG as the coordinating entity.

The operative principle, regardless of the size of the SMSA, is that growth policy decisions should be made by a unit with sufficient geographic coverage and responsibility to be able to address all or at least the most pertinent issues of trade-off within the region or commutershed. Thus in some cases counties will have responsibility for growth policy decisions; in other cases cities or combined city-counties are the logical locus of responsibility.

CONCLUSION

The preceding discussion of growth management responsibility has been presented in the form of descriptions of various levels of government. It is important to keep in mind that for any given piece of land or any geographic area the "policy" that determines the rate, character, and timing of development is the sum of all policies, programs, and actions of all governmental units as they together influence the decision-making process and the rights of the private landowner. Thus, growth policy in San Diego County, California, a county of approximately 1.4 million persons and 48,255 acres (roughly the size of Connecticut) is the composite of the policies and actions of 200 to 300 agencies (depending on the method of classification used), including 13 cities, one COG, one county government (with more than 30 agencies and departments influencing land development); more than 100 special districts; various state agencies; and federal involvement including the Border Patrol, Department of Transportation (DOT), HUD, EPA, Agriculture (Forest Service), and the U.S. Navy. Even in this relatively "manageable" region, management of growth forces is by no means a simple task. As noted above, some of the critical growth-inducing decisions are made at a distance from local decision makers. Alterations in the local composite "growth policy" are likely to be slow in coming, small in impact, and may often be offset or negated by shifts in other parts of the government network. At the present time, changes are occurring as the result of the gradual accretion of a large number of local policy changes in smaller jurisdictions. As we point out in the following chapters, the cumulative effect of these local actions may turn out to be more significant than the more highly publicized actions and proposals of higher levels of government.

NOTES

1. Kenneth Boulding, "The Economics of the Coming Spaceship Earth," in Environmental Quality in a Growing Economy ed., Henry Jarrett (Baltimore: Johns Hopkins Press, 1966).

2. D. H. Meadows et al., The Limits to Growth (New York: Universe Books, 1972).

3. Population and the American Future: Report of the Commission on Population Growth and the American Future (New York: New American Library, 1972).

4. U.S. Council on Environmental Quality (Bosselman and Callies), The Quiet Revolution in Land Use Controls (Washington, D.C.: U.S. Government Printing Office, 1971).

5. For a description of the Minnesota program, see American Society of Planning Officials, Minnesota's Fiscal Disparities Bill, Planning Advisory Service Memo No. M-9, February 1972.

CHANGING ATTITUDES
AND EMERGING ACTIONS

INDIVIDUAL LEVEL: PERSONAL CHOICE

It is easy to become overphilosophical about the individual roots
of the nongrowth movement. Reaching idealistic heights, one might
visualize a massive back-to-nature movement, with hordes of middle-
class suburban families and others taking their vast array of technological toys and electric gadgets to a central gathering place (perhaps
the nearest shopping-center parking lot) and setting fire to them as
cheers arise from the throng.

An even more basic part of the nongrowth movement, though,
is a rejection of hordes, of waiting in line, of taking a number, of being
classified by number, and of being allowed to make meaningful political
input only by random Gallup sample.

Some individual nongrowthers have probably already made some
adjustments in their own life styles and in those of their immediate
families. For example, they might transfer the television set to an
isolated sewing room, trade in the second car for a pair of bikes,
and make regular trips to the community recycling center instead of
to the home trash compactor.

Other individuals involved in nongrowth may have no specific
ideas about change or about cutting back. They may be suffering
almost daily psychic wounds from congested freeways, from indifferent
bureaucrats and service people, and from the rising level of general
background noise in their community. Some of these basic frustrations
and wounds may be priming individuals for a good dose of nongrowth
input. Individuals see a supposedly well-planned subdivision go up,
endure the mud and dust, and push their children into overcrowded
school buses. Often the planned parks and community centers never
see the light of day. Then taxes go up and entire tracts of homes
start deteriorating all at once. They may deteriorate even more quickly

15

if some planner forgot the area was in a flood plain, or if the planning commission chose to ignore the fact. The inhabitants of some rather remote subdivision cheer when they get their first filling station and drive-in restaurant, but then despair when it is followed by mile after mile of fast-food, fast-furniture, fast-muffler strip commercial developments.

To be realistic, the national life style will only drive a small minority to join hippie communes. But a central thesis of the nongrowth movement is that many people are either consciously or unconsciously disconcerted by the fruits of a few decades of rapid growth and are willing to act differently, vote differently, and maybe even pay more taxes to maintain a certain quality of life.

We feel that a lot more people would like to be able to predict their futures more accurately and to have some degree of control over change and their destinies. These feelings are shared by groups ranging from suburban bankers to the residents of black public-housing high-risers in the central city. They are shared by bigots as well— people who almost literally would like to grab a piece of territory and keep out all invaders. But for the most part, the supporters of nongrowth are individuals motivated by complex goals. There are black middle-class families, for example, who strongly resist the construction of housing in their suburbs or neighborhoods that would attract low-income blacks. There are young suburban professional couples who sincerely want to slow growth but just as sincerely want to accept at least a token amount of low-income housing.

COMMUNITY LEVEL: CHANGING POLITICS

Until recently, most communities viewed growth as a fairly natural, inevitable, and desirable phenomenon. Planners and decision makers often actively encouraged population and economic growth in their jurisdictions. Decline or even stability was viewed with concern. In the past few years, there has been a significant change in attitudes; a growing number of communities and political leaders have come right out and said "stop," or at least "slow down." The discussion of growth versus nongrowth is now out in the open in many areas, with the underlying assumption that future growth can be affected and perhaps even stopped as a matter of public policy. While the very mention of any form of nongrowth was enough to ensure political defeat several years ago, in many communities a planner or politican can now be criticized or defeated if he or she becomes too closely associated with a prodevelopment image.

Attitudes have been changing and hardening quite rapidly. Governor Tom McCall of Oregon had often been quoted in the early

1970s as telling people to come and visit his state but not to stay as permanent residents. But when he addressed a national convention of planners in 1973, he expressed strong doubts about even the temporary visitors:

> We've lately received a study from the Battelle Institute saying that by 1977 we won't be able to accommodate the tourists who will come to Oregon. How can Oregon—with a population of 2 million—plan for 10 million more who come here part-time? How can we keep the tourists from destroying what they came to enjoy? We're not inhospitable in Oregon. Everyone is welcome to visit us, but I'm not going out of my way to invite visitors if I think they will have to contend with shoulder-to-shoulder crowds.[1]

In our accelerated society, it appears as though local actions to control or stop growth are often moving ahead at a much faster pace than any real citizen participation and education efforts geared toward some basic attitude changes. In fact, this is one of the basic questions being asked of the nongrowth movement: When do you educate and when do you act?

There is a danger in acting too fast. It is fairly easy for a community to stop new housing from going up by putting a moratorium on the issuance of any more building permits or the approval of any more subdivision plans. This has already happened in various forms in places such as Aspen, Colorado; Livermore, California; Loudoun County, Virginia; and Dade County, Florida. There are many more tools that can be used and political, social, and economic actions that can be taken to keep out additional people and to keep growth and change at a minimum. But unless this is done with a general reservoir of support in the community and with some solid social, legal, and planning foundation, those responsible can soon find themselves facing lawsuits, court challenges, petitions, firings, and, if they are as unlucky as some Southern California planners, a meeting room full of angry construction workers.

On the other hand, planners and local citizens groups can quietly discuss future growth options for the community in plushly carpeted coffee-and-cake settings and generate rather minimal citizen interest and participation. This is generally because they appear to be almost powerless to implement any policies and no one feels threatened.

Sometimes discussion and research are seen as effective ways of channeling off or co-opting citizen nongrowth sentiment or general disgust with existing growth and change. This seemed to be the case in Ann Arbor, Michigan, a university community whose population

17

increased from 67,000 to almost 100,000 between 1960 and 1970. The citizens of Ann Arbor had been concerned about the ferment and sprawl associated with Detroit some 30 miles to the east. Then a series of annexations, the development of a new shopping center, and a temporary sewer crisis brought some of the more unpleasant aspects of growth to a head, and the city planning department was directed to undertake a nine-month study of the causes and effects of growth.

The resulting 435-page document,[2] one of the longest local nongrowth studies published to date anywhere in the country, appears to present every bit of data the staff could uncover relative to growth. "When we started, the city council wanted us to concentrate on facts and not work in any opinions," one of the city planners said when asked why there was such a lack of policy orientation. "But later on, things changed as new members were elected to the council. Now nobody wants to read all those statistics—they want policies and concrete recommendations." Then, late in 1973, the planning director resigned to accept a position with the developers of the new shopping center that had started much of the concern. Ann Arbor continues to grow as attitudes and actions fail to focus on one set of policies.

The key to the "action or education" question at the local level is probably to maintain a point of dynamic tension between the quiet voice of the educator and the power thrusts of a Saul Alinsky or Ralph Nader. Guidelines on appropriate strategies will be presented later in the book.

GOVERNMENT ACTIONS

It is difficult to estimate the total number of communities and regions that have taken some sort of public action to consciously slow or stop growth. A "List of Areas with Growth Constraints"[3] was distributed by the Urban Land Institute in March 1973. This list contained a total of 39 counties, cities, and townships, with another seven listed as possible candidates. In addition, the list contained the names of five states—Delaware, Hawaii, New Hampshire, Oregon, and Vermont. Maine and Colorado were listed as possible candidates.

We estimate that there are more than 100 cities and regions that have seriously considered slowing or stopping growth as a matter of public policy. There could easily be twice that many or more. Without any real central clearinghouse of nongrowth actions, the news of such communities is usually communicated by word of mouth at professional conferences, in magazine and newspaper articles, and by various reports that list court decisions. Some growth-challenging communities such as Ramapo, New York, get a lot of publicity because their strategies have been tested and evaluated in detail in the courts and in the legal literature. Others, such as Eugene, Oregon; Tucson, Arizona; Boise, Idaho; and Aurora, Colorado, have received much less attention and analysis at the national level, possibly because their programs remain in less widely circulated local plan form.

While the number of real nongrowth activists is a rather small fraction of the total number of communities and regions in the United States, it should be noted that for every one community taking direct action, there are at least three or four more cautiously observing, researching, and preparing for action. In addition, the authors have found that nongrowth activity seems more likely to occur when one or more of the following factors are present: (1) a university town, (2) a generally high income level, (3) rapid growth in the past, (4) a history of poor planning or no planning, and (5) location in a fragile environmental area. Thus, a search for significant nongrowth actions might be the most fruitful if conducted in certain areas—say, in university towns and upper-income suburbs in the western United States or in urbanizing coastal or mountain areas. However, there are always such exceptions as Garden Grove, California, and Dane County, Wisconsin, which show that growth can also be an issue in middle-income areas or in the rather flat Midwest. Some of the black residents of Los Angeles, Seattle, and Chicago's South and West sides have been opposing new expressways and excessive densities in ghetto areas, thus adding another dimension to the nongrowth movement.

There is no doubt that the combined weight of local and regional nongrowth actions has been heavy, heavier, in fact, than it would appear when one looks at any one case in detail. Yet to challenge growth as such is a new and controversial idea. To challenge it in growth-impacted areas that have been growing more rapidly than the rest of the state or the country can result in especially heated controversy.

For a national overview of changing attitudes on growth and emerging implementation techniques, it is necessary to do quite a bit of traveling through both time and space.

The movement toward nongrowth at the local and regional level started in the late 1960s, but significant actions were not reported until the 1970s. In fact, by the end of 1973 not one community in the country had really acted to stop growth cold as a matter of public policy. Few if any had even implemented a full range of actions to seriously slow growth below previous rates. This is not meant to disparage the many serious and potentially effective local and regional studies and experiments in this direction. Total nongrowth or instant nongrowth is a very difficult policy to implement. Nongrowth with real social equity or regional responsibility is even more difficult, but it is essential on both moral and legal grounds. We feel that the extreme ideas of completely stopping growth and actively redistributing resources should have considerably more public exposure, rather than being discussed in a clandestine atmosphere.

19

If local communities have the right to be different, if they have the right to provide their residents with the highest possible quality of life, then it would seem logical that not all communities have the legal obligation to grow in the "Los Angeles manner." (It is interesting to note, in this connection, that recent city general plan hearings seem to indicate that Los Angeles itself does not want to "grow like Los Angeles" anymore.) This is a fundamental concern of many nongrowth advocates, one which seems to be overlooked by many critics, especially critics in the legal profession. They would leave it to the developers and to our mobile population to determine which communities should grow and at what rate they should develop. While the movers and developers are making up their minds, these critics would require all communities to leave their doors open. For example, Chicago attorney and land use expert Fred Bosselman strongly objected when the highest court in the state of New York upheld the rather mild but comprehensive Ramapo, New York, development-timing ordinance. In an article entitled "Can the Town of Ramapo Pass a Law to Bind the Rights of the Whole World?", Bosselman wrote:

> In 1969 the town of Ramapo, New York, adopted a relatively new legal technique that allows local governments to limit severely the amount of new residential development. This technique, known generally as "development timing," gives local government an even more powerful tool for determining who will live within its borders than had heretofore been available.
>
> This article expresses the opinion that, based on past experience, each town can be expected to exercise this and similar techniques as if it were an island independent of other towns: that the resulting impact on metropolitan growth patterns will have serious social and environmental consequences; and that the laws of individual towns and cities, such as Ramapo, must not be allowed to bind the whole world without adequate state supervision.[4]

What Bosselman and others fail to note is that Ramapo merely wanted to stretch out a complete buildup of its area from the expected "natural" period of nine years to a "planned" period of 18 years. There never was a question of stopping growth completely. Quite to the contrary, Ramapo has a capital improvements program to provide the necessary public facilities to accommodate all growth within the 18-year period.

But what is going to happen to Ramapo at the end of the 18 years, when the town is all built up with the expected single-family homes?

Does Ramapo then have an obligation to accommodate developers proposing high-rise apartments? Is the town obliged to grow indefinitely?

In a related example, the San Francisco Bay area city of Petaluma was defeated in an early 1974 federal court battle to establish annual quotas for future housing construction (approximately 500 units a year) and to establish locational and qualitative criteria to be considered in the allotment of the quota. The construction industry charged the city with everything from "placing a unique and undue burden on new housing construction," to a "radical departure" from the past national policy of "free demographic trends" or the right to travel. The authors feel that a growth rate of 500 units a year is realistic, given Petaluma's population, land area, and fiscal and administrative resources. The figure of 500 units corresponds fairly well with the annual construction rate of new residences in the past decade. But construction interests and other critics of nongrowth once again see any attempt to tamper with the "natural" rate of growth as illegal, even when the natural rate for a growth-impacted community has been much higher than the overall regional, state, or national average.

According to one newspaper account of the court battle, the suit against Petaluma (filed by the Construction Industry Association of Sonoma County; the San Francisco, Peninsula, and Redwood Empire Building Industry Association; Petaluma Partners; and William Lawrence), "is being closely watched by city officials throughout the state. Its outcome will affect similar laws now being considered." The same account also quoted a Petaluma city planner, who noted that the growth control plan worked well in its first year of operation. He said that instead of creating vast subdivisions with matching houses, builders were presenting plans that left green belts around clusters of homes. Another city official said that "All of a sudden we've had an impressive array of builders competing for the [available] allocations."

EMERGING TECHNIQUES TO CONTROL GROWTH

We could not find a single community that aimed all its ordinances and policies at stopping growth cold or holding it at some immediate level deemed optimal, although some suburban officials in Chicago and elsewhere are willing to speak about such policies off the record. Few communities have dared to set ultimate limits on either land area or population; the more common tactic is to try to slow down the rate of development with no ultimate goal in mind.

Development staging and phasing is not all that new, despite what Bosselman said in his critique of Ramapo's legislation. In the

21

1950s, some of Ramapo's neighbors in Rockland County, namely Clarkstown and Orangeville, each adopted somewhat similar development scheduling ordinances, limiting the number of homes that could be developed to coincide with available school capacity.[5] The Clarkstown ordinance, like Ramapo's, stressed lower-density residential areas, requiring that lots in the outlying area of the community be no smaller than one acre; but unlike Ramapo, Clarkstown permitted more intensive development if the developer could prove that the project would not overburden schools and community facilities.[6]

A newer technique, one more uniquely related to the nongrowth movement, is the "population cap." Citizens can petition to put a desired optimum population for the community on the ballot, as they did in Boulder, Colorado, in November 1971. In this case, the resolution on the ballot sought to "stabilize the ultimate population of the city of Boulder near one hundred thousand," compared to the 1971 population of about 70,000.

Once again, this resolution did not seek to stop growth completely, even though it was heavily backed by the local chapter of Zero Population Growth. The city could have grown by more than 40 percent of its 1971 population. In addition, Boulder had grown by 80 percent between 1960 and 1970, a rate which was three times higher than that of the state as a whole. But the resolution was defeated by Boulder voters by a six-to-four ratio. Another resolution calling for a study of optimal city growth was approved by more than 70 percent of the voters. The results of this study will be covered in Chapter 3, which is devoted to Boulder.

Another example of a population cap is the one approved in November 1972 by voters in Boca Raton, Florida, a fairly wealthy community of some 40,000. The ordinance limits the optimum population by limiting the total number of housing units to 40,000. This would work out to an ultimate population of 100,000, which is about 150 percent more than the present population.

Rather than trying to stop population growth by local public policy, or "using zoning as a contraceptive," as one attorney put it, other communities have tried to practice nongrowth by putting some optimal limits on their area. The most common form this strategy takes is the establishment of some kind of "urban limit line," usually by stating that sewers, water, and other facilities will not be extended beyond a certain boundary or that further annexations will be denied beyond some point. While at first glance this would appear to be less controversial than trying to put a limit on population growth, areas that have proposed such strategies—such as Sacramento County, California; Boise, Idaho; and Salem, Oregon—have encountered strong opposition, primarily based on the assertion that land prices would go sky high within the urban limit line and down to almost zero outside the line.

22

It is important to remember that an urban limit line has two sides. Communities have been using the technique both to contain urbanization (inside) and to protect agricultural land, open space, and lower-density development (outside). Since in many cases the impact of an urban limit line is felt most sharply at the fringe, near the edge of a metropolitan area, some feel that there should be an evaluation of the regional impact of such proposals. Unfortunately, regional mechanisms for both evaluation and enforcement of urban limit lines do not exist in many areas.

Planners are generally more willing to accept urban limit lines than population cap measures, since the former represent a logical extension of traditional planning concerns about greenbelts, preservation of agricultural lands, higher-density central cities, capital improvement policies, consolidation of development around transportation facilities, and the general prevention of urban sprawl. The concept of a floating or flexible urban limit line, already adopted in Eugene, Oregon, and Manatee County, Florida, is an even safer bet for planners. Eugene's line, which is being adopted in stages, seems more flexible in that it will be periodically reviewed and expanded when necessary. Manatee County's line, adopted in January 1973, is extremely flexible, being based on the "ripple" concept—that is, the concept of growth moving out into the undeveloped rural areas in successive rings, much as a ripple moves across a body of water. The Manatee County line can be penetrated by rezonings and subdivisions if the developments will generally pay their way in terms of municipal services; thus Mantatee's policy serves more as a cost-revenue technique than as a real urban limit line.

In Oregon's Willamette Valley (Salem area), the Mid-Willamette Valley Council of Governments proposed a more firm urban limit line in June 1971 as part of a new comprehensive plan. A boundary line was drawn around an area containing approximately 71 square miles, compared with the 27 square miles within the Salem city limits at that time. The council recommended that the area outside and adjacent to the boundary should be retained as a buffer zone between the central city and the rural agricultural areas through the use of sewer and water extension policies, parks, permanently zoned agricultural lands, and preservation of open space. The plan met with heavy opposition from real estate interests and landowners outside the line.

Despite the opposition, the planners kept working on the proposal and prepared an impressive number of background studies on the economic, legal, governmental, and environmental aspects of the line. In August 1973 an agreement adopting six urban growth policies was signed by Polk County, Marion County, and the city of Salem. One of the policies was that "an urban growth boundary shall be established by the parties hereto and said parties shall take the necessary action to have the boundary and the policies herein set forth made a part of their respective comprehensive plans."

Thus it can be seen that controlling future population growth in any kind of absolute terms at the local level is a rare event, one which may result in defeat at the polls or a trip to court. The core of the argument against such actions is that the nation will experience a lot of inevitable growth in the future and that if such growth is not accommodated in one place it will have to go elsewhere. To the extent that this is true, widespread nongrowth could restrict the mobility of the poor who are searching for better jobs and decent housing. But most of the people who use such arguments are not demographers. It is interesting to note that even demographers tend to disagree on how much future growth is really inevitable.[7] In the following quotation, attorney Fred Bosselman provides a somewhat overstated summary of the argument against growth:

> That the imposition of local limitations on growth is a foolish response to a serious problem seems so self-evident that it would be hardly necessary to spend time arguing the point were it not for the tremendous increase within the past year of the popularity of the stop-growth movement. Obviously, the overall growth of the nation depends on the number of people who are born, immigrate, emigrate and die. Stopping the growth of Livermore (California) or Boulder or Palm Beach does not reduce the nation's population growth; it merely directs it somewhere else. While it may be in the self-interest of the existing residents of a particular municipality to divert the problems caused by growth onto other areas and other people, it is fraudulent to justify this diversion on the grounds of environmental improvement unless some impartial source has evaluated the environmental impact of the various alternatives. The wolf of exclusionary zoning hides under the environmental sheepskin worn by the stop-growth movement.[8]

Yet if communities do have a right to be different, it does seem that there might be many legitimate reasons for directing the "inevitable growth" elsewhere. Under traditional zoning enabling legislation, which seeks to protect the public health, safety, and general welfare, a rather general desire to keep things the way they are might not yet be considered as sufficient reason for stopping growth. Even so, the aspects that determine the quality of life of a community are receiving much more attention in planning and legal circles, and a community may eventually be able to stop rapid growth and constant change in order to protect the psychological well-being of its present and future residents. For the more immediate future, it still seems that there are physical environmental factors, if nothing else, that should provide reason enough for some communities to grow quite a bit and others to grow not at all, or even to decline. Environmental carrying capacity studies have been slow to surface as a basis for local or even regional nongrowth efforts. There are a number of reasons for this, including the fact that such studies are expensive and that jurisdictional boundaries often do not correspond with various natural features and systems. It is also easier and quicker for a community to base nongrowth actions on cost-revenue studies or some other rather simple impacts of growth, such as traffic congestion, overcrowded schools, or loss of agricultural land.

Ultimately, communities might have the opportunity to be different and to pursue different styles of life only if a comprehensive national population growth and distribution policy is adopted. The national response to local nongrowth actions and attitudes is explored in Chapter 1. But as of 1973, there has still been no real national response on these vital questions. The question then becomes, What can and should localities and regions do on their own? Should they act as if such policies were in effect at the national and state levels and avoid taking the matter into their own hands? Or should they go ahead and act, however reluctantly, on the premise that local action with some concern for social justice and regional impacts is better than nothing? This, in fact, is the major practical nongrowth question local and regional governments now face.

NOTES

1. Governor Tom McCall, Plenary Session speech to the National Planning Conference of the American Society of Planning Officials, Los Angeles, April 9, 1973.

2. Ann Arbor Planning Department, The Ann Arbor Growth Study (Ann Arbor, Mich., 1972).

3. For more information on this list and on related research on the nongrowth issue, contact the Urban Land Institute, 1200 18th St., N.W., Washington, D.C. 20036.

4. Fred P. Bosselman, "Can the Town of Ramapo Pass a Law to Bind the Rights of the Whole World?", Florida State University Law Review 1 (1973): 234–235.

5. Mel Scott, American City Planning Since 1890 (Berkeley: University of California Press, 1969): 508–510.

6. For a description of this ordinance, see Josephs v. Clarkstown, 24 Misc. 2d 336, 198 N.Y.S. 2d 695 (Sup. Ct., Rockland County, 1960).

7. See, for example, George Grier, <u>The Baby Bust</u> (Washington, D.C.: The Washington Center for Metropolitan Studies, 1971). Grier makes the point that zero population growth or even actual decline could be achieved in the United States in a few decades, perhaps within the present century.

8. Bosselman, op. cit., pp. 248-249.

BOULDER, COLORADO:
AN INNOVATIVE
NONGROWTH COMMUNITY

In early 1972, Boulder was probably the most advanced city in the country when it came to a public consciousness that growth can be controlled or significantly affected as a matter of public policy. But by the end of 1973, the city had done a lot more studying and the momentum had slowed. Sandra Cooper, the chairman of the Boulder Area Growth Study Commission, made the following comments when the commissioned 10-volume report was released in December 1973:

> We didn't lose our courage as a community. The growth study commission was very unhappy to see how few options we had regarding the control of future growth. It was like hearing there was no Santa Claus. I'm exhausted.

What happened in Boulder during those two years of heavy activity and study in the area of nongrowth? The answer requires a much more detailed look at this innovative community and a wider time frame of observation.

BACKGROUND: A RAPIDLY
GROWING COMMUNITY

Boulder, Colorado, a university town with a population of about 74,000, nestled on the east side of the Rocky Mountains about 25 miles northwest of Denver, has been described as the Camelot of the nongrowth movement. Some civic leaders have called it "the nicest town in America," and other residents hesitate to praise it in public only because they fear that more people will want to move there.

———————

This chapter was prepared by Earl Finkler.

The fear of rapid in-migration is well founded. The city's population has almost doubled from some 20,000 in 1950 to about 38,000 in 1960. Since 1960 it has almost doubled again. During 1960-70, Boulder grew about three times faster than the state of Colorado as a whole.

While Boulder has been described as a Camelot, without its outstanding natural setting it would probably look more like a Levittown. There is an early history of planning in the community dating back to 1910 when a local civic association hired Frederick Law Olmsted, Jr., to prepare a city plan. However, the period of rapid growth in the 1950s and early 1960s appears to have overwhelmed many plans. The downtown section is congested, with scattered blight and a need for more parking. There is a crossroads of strip and related commercial uses on the outskirts, which had the room but not the overall planning coordination to develop into a shopping center. Actually, there is no regional shopping center in the Boulder area. When one was proposed recently and backed by the planning staff, the citizens rose up and defeated the proposed annexation needed to accommodate the development. The citizens apparently felt that the shopping center would cause more growth, congestion, and pollution, and would strike a fatal blow to the downtown area. These concerns outweighed some of the more positive aspects, such as increased shopping opportunities.

Boulder has an advantage in its very strong citizenry, above average in education and income and with a keen appreciation for the natural setting and their ability to have a say in community decisions. The city has an excellent planning staff. William Lamont, who became director in 1967, achieved some substantial planning breakthroughs primarily on the force of his long identification with the area and personal approach to citizens and community leaders. Unfortunately, Lamont resigned at the end of 1973, as did his assistant director. But the initiative in Boulder's recent growth-challenging efforts and the recently released Growth Study Commission report has been in the hands of the citizens, not the planners. In my opinion, this is the key to what has happened in Boulder. Planners and citizens across the country are currently getting in touch with each other and devising all sorts of citizen participation schemes to handle the controversial new topic of nongrowth. Boulder has been doing this for some time, and the results should be of national interest, despite the rather defensive posture of the chairman of the Growth Study Commission, Sandra Cooper, who told me that "In terms of national recognition [of Boulder's growth study], I don't give a damn. We did the study for the city and county of Boulder, not the nation."

In studying communities that have challenged growth, I have noticed that they have usually been aroused to concern and action by some traumatic event or series of events. In Orange County, California, for example, it was the incorporation and development of the major new community of Irvine. In Ann Arbor, Michigan, the city council kept approving developments until it was suddenly discovered that the sewage treatment facilities were overloaded.

In Boulder, one of the big traumatic events appears to have been IBM's massive purchase of 640 acres of land in the late 1950s for a new plant, developed in the mid-1960s in an area known as Gunbarrel. Since IBM moved into the unincorporated area, which lies several miles from the Boulder city limits, residential and commercial uses have followed suit, and there is presently a controversy over whether the area should incorporate or be annexed by Boulder. In the early 1960s the city had a "spokes of the wheel" policy, which extended services along major arteries radiating out from the center of the city. When IBM assembled its land outside the city and asked for sewer and water, a special district was formed to provide the services, with some financial assistance from the company.

As one report on the subject noted:

The intent at the time was that the Gunbarrel-Heatherwood community would be annexed [by Boulder] within three or four years. . . . But this did not occur.

Eight years later in 1973 there are still three-and-a-half miles of undeveloped land between Gunbarrel and the edge of the city, making annexation in the near future unlikely. [State law requires that one-sixth of the area to be annexed be contiguous to the city.] This community has 8,000 people today and a potential of growing to 30,000 or more. It has urban density, but it lacks urban type policy and fire facilities. This lack combined with the heavy water service charges (double the in-city rate) has caused the residents to seek some change in their status.

The Spokes of the Wheel policy was successful in controlling the quality of new development along the spokes but it failed to confine new development to these areas. Subdividers in other parts of the valley were able to obtain water from other sources.[1]

There have been other less traumatic but more cumulative developments in Boulder. One planner said that the number of automobiles and vehicles has been increasing at a faster rate than the population. In addition, the community has always been concerned with protecting its mountain backdrop. As far back as 1912, Olmsted urged the residents to reject a roller coaster and amusement park on Flagstaff Mountain. The citizens acted to carry out Olmsted's recommendation. In 1962, a resort hotel was proposed for a mesa overlooking Boulder. The land was purchased by the city to block the development. The now-famous greenbelt acquisition was initiated by the city in 1967, when the voters approved a referendum earmarking 40 percent of the new second-cent sales tax to preserve natural areas, primarily in the mountain backdrop. From 1968 to 1972, the greenbelt program enabled the city to acquire 2,740 acres through purchase or option. The sales tax revenues pour in about $600,000 a year to the greenbelt program, but it is estimated that it would take $15 to $26 million to accomplish the entire program. Thus, in the November 1971 election the voters made it possible to use $5.5 million in revenue bonds as an additional source of open-space financing. The first $2 million worth of bonds were sold in January 1973.

CITIZENS VOTE FOR A STUDY OF GROWTH

As the 1960s turned into the 1970s, Boulder started to develop a rather remarkable array of growth management tools, many with the assistance of planning director William Lamont. These tools were described in some detail in my American Society of Planning Officials report on nongrowth,[2] but perhaps one of the most important is the use of "plant investment fees." These are one-time fees for tapping on to water and sewer lines. The fees vary according to the type of unit. For example, it costs a single family house $950 for water and $450 for sewers. Fees for commercial and industrial developments are based on the size of pipe required. The city has agreed to exempt or discount these rates in the case of some federally subsidized housing.

But perhaps the high point in Boulder's campaign against growth came in the local elections in November 1971. The local chapter of Zero Population Growth had circulated petitions, turning in more than 1,700 signatures, and it succeeded in placing on the ballot a charter amendment "to stabilize the ultimate population of the city of Boulder near one hundred thousand," compared to the population of about 70,000 at the end of 1971. The proposal was favored by some 41.5 percent of the voters, but this was not enough to pass it. A companion resolution, sponsored by the city council, was approved by more than 70 percent of the voters. This resolution directed the city to:

Undertake a definitive analysis of the optimum population and growth rate for the Boulder Valley [and, in the meantime, to] take all steps necessary to hold the rate of growth in the Boulder Valley to a level substantially below that experienced in the 1960s.

Boulder was probably the first city in the nation to put an optimum population figure on the ballot. Even though the specific ZPG proposal did not pass, the antigrowth forces felt they were sending a message to the rest of the country. "If the Boulder [ZPG] resolution had passed last November, the underlying theology of growth in this country would have been significantly questioned," state legislator Richard Lamm told me in April 1972.

The ZPG amendment was only the tip of the iceberg. The same November 1971 election had produced four new city councilmen, two of whom had supported the amendment. In the following February the city discouraged new primary employment centers from locating in the Boulder Valley. The city was also directed to "request other city, county, and federal agencies, both public and private, to refrain from promoting the Boulder Valley for the location of such centers."

Boulder was riding a real nongrowth crest in the early months of 1972. Planning director William Lamont estimated in April 1972 that his department had received over 70 inquiries regarding various aspects of nongrowth from planners and individuals all over the country. Planners from other university communities such as Ann Arbor, Michigan, visited Boulder to take back some firsthand impressions and information. Lamont was in great demand as a speaker, appearing on several programs at the national planning conference of the American Society of Planning Officials in Detroit in April 1972.

But the major achievement of the November 1971 election, at least in the minds of many Boulder citizens, was the "definitive" growth study called for by the voters. Right from the start, it was determined that this was to be a citizen's study, not one done by planners, technical experts, and outside consultants, as has been the case in a number of other communities that have since challenged growth. A nine-member citizens' study committee was appointed by the city council in October 1971 to lay out the broad outline for the growth study. The text of their document is reproduced as an appendix to my ASPO nongrowth report.[3]

The basic outline of a major study is perhaps the most important step, as any scholar knows. It is important to decide right from the start not only the precise questions that will be covered but to eliminate the many and diverse questions that will not. The citizens' study committee raised many questions. "This looks like the outline for a very comprehensive master plan," one planner in the ASPO Chicago office told me after reviewing the document. And so it was—the document covered physical, ecological, aesthetic, political, legal, demographic, economic, and social factors. In addition, some rather quick policy determinations were made by the study committee, including the following conclusions:

Limiting or managing population growth is not in itself
a long-term goal: it is a way of gaining other benefits
. . . . The analysis will miss the mark if it focuses
initially on optimum city size and financial efficiency or
the area within the city limits alone.[4]

There was also heavy emphasis on citizen participation, including
some references to the effect that the process of citizen consultation
and education would be as important, if not more important, than the
product of the written growth study.

With the completion of this wide-ranging outline, the city council
and county commissioners appointed a formal 13-member growth-
study commission in April 1972. A comprehensive planning assistance
grant for two-thirds of the $100,000 growth study budget was approved
by the Department of Housing and Urban Development (HUD) in the
fall of 1972. The city and Boulder County provided the rest of the
money. This was probably the first HUD 701 planning grant in the
country to be used for a study of growth versus nongrowth. There
were high hopes for the Boulder growth study, not only in the city,
but also in the HUD Denver office and in many places across the
nation. Boulder clearly had an advantage over many other communities starting to consider nongrowth as a planning alternative. In the
fall of 1972, Boulder also had HUD money to study optimal population
size—almost $1.00 per capita. Then the fun began.

A DISAPPOINTING STUDY

The unfortunate fact is that the Boulder Area Growth Study Commission appears to have bungled part of its assignment and to have
slowed the growth-challenging momentum of the community. Of
course opinions vary on this matter, as I discovered during a three-
day follow-up field trip to Boulder in December 1973. The ponderous
10-volume report of the commission was impossible to analyze in
great detail in time to meet the deadline for this book. But I did talk
to a number of Boulder residents (including the commission chairman
and one other member of that body) about the report and the track
record of the commission. I also discussed the commission's work
with the chairman of Boulder Zero Population Growth, Boulder planning director William Lamont, and Emmett Haywood, a planning and
management officer with the Department of Housing and Urban Development in Denver. Haywood, a former Boulder city planner, was the
HUD official primarily responsible for financing and administering
the study.

I also read all or part of six of the commission volumes, including the official commission report and recommendations. My

negative conclusions about the commission reflect my national perspective on local nongrowth activity. Ever since I first visited Boulder on nongrowth field research in April 1972, I felt that this might really be the community to send a strong, well-formulated antigrowth message to the nation. There was a spirit of adventure, of civic innovation in Boulder in early 1972. But by the end of 1973 the community had lost not only its planning director but also most of its national leadership role in the field of challenging growth. The project director for the study was gone, having left as soon as the one-year funding ran out, and the citizens on the commission were scattered and tired, with no plans for any coordinated effort at implementation. This suggests that the commission had a rather negative impact not only on the national but also on the local scene, although by the end of 1973 the local impact was extremely difficult to gauge.

Andrew Briscoe, a member of the commission, disagreed to some extent with my conclusion. "Some good came out from the study in that it happened," he said in an interview during my visit in December 1973. "Even if no one reads the report, the effort was worth it," he said. "People were exposed to many aspects of growth management. The environment for growth management has improved," he added.

On the other hand, Briscoe said he was generally unhappy with the study. He said the commission set out to do an "undoable" task and that they had underestimated the amount of staff work to be done, including the work done by consultants. "We did the study almost external to government—we went too far that way," he said. According to Briscoe, the original concept of the study was that it should be "of the people, by the people, and for the people." But he noted that this approach alienated the city government, especially the planning office. "There was a great landslide of emotional citizen volunteers at first," he said, "but that died out fairly soon and there was still a lot of hard work to be done."

I asked Briscoe if the citizens had placed too much reliance on professors and other consultants from the University of Colorado. When I visited Boulder in April 1972 I was told by a number of citizens that outside consultants were not needed because local people and University of Colorado experts could handle all the necessary work. In fact, with the exception of a land use consulting firm from Denver, almost all of the work was done by locals, especially university members.

"The university effort was very good," Briscoe said, "but we got started late and got only one semester of work instead of two as we had planned. Some professors had depended on two semesters of student help when they volunteered for the growth study, but this was cut back due to our late start."

Two of the major conclusions in the volume on the commission's final report are (1) that it is extremely difficult or impossible for any municipality in Boulder County to completely control its own destiny, and (2) that the one real population limitation model studied by the commission would be severely exclusionary and would be found unacceptable by the courts, even though this model calculated a population gain from the Boulder Valley base of 88,000 in 1973 to 112,000 by 1990. The 1990 population in the three other models studied ranged from 160,000 in a continuation of current policies and trends to 205,000 for the model emphasizing social, cultural, and economic diversity.

The final report strongly emphasizes the lack of local power to determine optimum growth. Briscoe emphasized the point:

> Local government has disgustingly little power over its own future. We are hooked together with the whole world. Most of the growth decision makers are external to our city limits. For example, IBM and Kodak didn't ask us to come into the area.

Yet when I asked Briscoe where I could find the documentation for such a major conclusion, he was rather vague. "I think we documented it as best we can. We almost all believed that to be the case," he said. The commission chairman, Sandra Cooper, backed up Briscoe on this point, saying "If there's urban sprawl all around Boulder, what are we going to gain as a city? There is strong influence for growth coming from outside Boulder. We've got to recognize this." Yet she didn't seem able to back up this point with hard documentation, although she did say that all the consultants made basically the same finding and emphasized to the commission how hopeless it would be for Boulder to go it alone.

Regarding possible court challenges resulting from commission recommendations for future growth control activities in Boulder, Cooper said the commission felt it would not be necessary to go to court. She said this could be avoided if Boulder would cooperate with the county and the other municipalities in the area. But she did note that the mayor of Boulder had said only recently that the city was not afraid to be hauled into court.

Did the Boulder Area Growth Study Commission become intimidated from attempting any radical challenge to growth as their initial momentum slowed and they became weighted down by information and opinions from their university consultants? I put the question to Emmett Haywood of HUD. He avoided giving any definitive opinion on the commission report when we talked in December 1973, saying that HUD was still in the process of reviewing the volumes. But he did note that the study was undertaken as a kind of cooperative venture between the city and county, with some amount of state interest as well. "This could have been one reason the subject matter had to be handled carefully and delicately," he said.

FINDINGS OF THE COMMISSION

The complete report of the commission takes up 10 volumes, with a total of 1,711 pages, hardly an easy afternoon's reading. The volumes were offered for sale in December 1973 from the City of Boulder, Department of Community Development, Box 791, Boulder, Colorado 80302. The prices for individual volumes varied from $3.18 to $10.68, with a package deal for the complete set offered at $58.28.

A summary of the individual volumes follows:

Boulder Area Growth Study

Vol. I. Commission Final Report ($3.18).
This volume contains the findings and recommendations of the Boulder Area Growth Study Commission based upon its analysis of the reports provided the Commission by its consultants. 151 pages.

Vol. II. Economic-Demographic Projections ($9.65)
This volume contains the research and recommendations provided by the Economic-Demographic Consultants to the study. The report analyzes and interrelates aspects of economic activity and population in Boulder County. 292 pages.
Consultants: Charles W. Howe, John Holt, and Jay April.

Vol. III. Environmental Constraints and Opportunities ($10.68).
This volume contains the report from the Environmental Constraints and Opportunities Consultant and two related papers. The major report provides an environmental inventory and land use recommendations for Boulder County. The papers describe two new mapping techniques—computerized mapping and photomorphic mapping. 274 pages with maps.
Consultant: Richard F. Madole.
Papers by: George Nez and Janey E. Nichol.

Vol. IV. Land Use Aspects ($9.47).
This volume summarizes land use planning aspects for Boulder County. Reports on the findings and recommendations of the Housing Consultant, Utilities

Technical Advisory Team, and Transportation Con-
sultant are incorporated within the report by the Land
Use Planning Consultants. 188 pages with maps.
Land Use Consultants: Beardsley, David
                        Associates, Inc.
                        Colorado Housing, Inc.
Housing Consultants:
Utilities Technical
    Advisory Team: David Harrison,
                        Chairman
Transportation Con-
    sultant: William A. Ganter

Vol. V.   Public Finance and Optimum Size:
          Business Conditions ($5.35).
                   This volume contains the reports from the Public
                   Finance and Optimum Size Consultants and the Busi-
                   ness Conditions Consultants. The Public Finance and
                   Optimum Size Report analyzes and forecasts revenues
                   and expenditures in the City of Boulder with reference
                   to future growth patterns and optimum city size. "Busi-
                   ness Conditions" comments from a business point of
                   view on the four model futures selected by the Com-
                   mission for research purposes. 147 pages.
          Public Finance and Optimum
                Size Consultants: David E. Dowall
                                   Nicholas W. Schrock
                                   Larry D. Singell
          Business Conditions
                Consultants: William H. Baughn
                                   Philip R. Cateora
                                   Lawrence D. Coolidge

Vol. VI. Legal-Political Aspects:Economic
          Incentives and Disincentives ($6.86).
                   This volume contains the reports from the Legal-
                   Political Consultants and the Economic Incentives
                   and Disincentives Consultants. The first section
                   contains six papers on legal issues relating to growth
                   control; the last section, a paper on tax devices to con-
                   trol growth. 196 pages.
          Legal-Political Consultants: Stephen F. Williams and
                                       Donald M. Carmichael
          Business Incentives and
                Disincentives Con-
                sultants: David Seckler and
                                     Paul Huszar

Vol. VII.   Solid Waste ($3.62).
                 This volume contains the Solid Waste report written
                 for the Commission by its consultants. The report
                 analyzes and forecasts solid waste generation and
                 disposal for the four model futures selected by the
                 Commission for research purposes. 75 pages with
                 maps.
             Consultants: P. J. Giarratano, R. C. Hess,
                             B. J. Kaiser, and M. E. Sehnert.
Vol. VIII. Social and Humanistic Aspects ($5.73).
                 This volume contains the report from the Sociology
                 Consultants and analyzes sociological factors relating
                 to the four model futures selected by the Commission
                 for research purposes. The Humanistic section
                 reproduces lectures presented to the public by hu-
                 manities scholars during the Forum on Growth, a
                 two-week community consultation. 165 pages.
             Consultants: N. A. Hilmar and M. S. Baur
             Humanities lecturers: Kenneth Boulding, Gilbert
                                     White, Charley George, James
                                     Burbank, Ren Paget, David
                                     Hawkins, and Stan Brakhage
Vol. IX.   Judgments About Growth ($4.55).
                 This volume contains the reports from the Con-
                 sultants on Judgments about Growth. These reports
                 are: a summary of Boulder Goals compiled from
                 various goals studies; and, two papers relating to
                 how judgments about growth are made. 129 pages.
             Consultants: Derick O. Steinmann, Thomas K. Stewart,
                             and Kenneth R. Hammond.
Vol. X.   Summary ($3.98).
                 This volume is a compilation of summaries authored
                 for the Commission by its consultants. Each summary
                 appears in the related volume. Summaries from the
                 following reports are included in this volume: Final
                 Commission Report, Economic-Demographic Pro-
                 jections, Environmental Constraints and Opportunities,
                 Land Use Aspects, Public Finance and Optimum Size,
                 Legal-Political Aspects, Solid Waste, and Judgments
                 about Growth. 94 pages.

     As noted previously, it will be impossible to examine each
volume in any detail. However, the general consensus of the local
people I spoke with in December 1973 seemed to indicate that the
best volumes were V, dealing with Public Finance and Optimum Size:

Business Conditions and VI, especially the part on Legal - Political Aspects.

William Lamont had his city planning staff analyze the first six volumes that were published. A different staff member was assigned to read each volume. The staff comments follow:

Vol. II.   Economic-Demographic Projections
            Few conclusions/little value. Question whether model can be adjusted to permit simulation by playing with variables.
Vol. III.   Environmental Constraints and Opportunities
            Good inventory at a generalized level. Needs specificity before usable. An introduction, but no direct implementation—rather, highlights what should be studied.
Vol. IV.   Land Use Aspects
            Good summary of the issues.
Vol. V.   Public Finance and Optimum Size: Business Conditions
            Seems like best.
Vol. VII.   Solid Waste
            Why single it out? Poor, weak.
Vol. VIII. Social and Humanistic Aspects
            No data, no innovative suggestions—philosophical orientation.
Vol. IX.   Judgments about Growth
            Good analysis of surveys done last number of years. The section on citizens' judgment about Boulder is the poorest of the three. The conclusions add nothing to present knowledge.

William Toner (who wrote the Introduction to Nongrowth Economics in this volume) took a look at Volume V, Public Finance and Optimum Size. He concluded that there was no analysis of the structure and functioning of the local economy, a structure which he said will play the most significant role in Boulder's economic future.

According to Toner, "The large policy choices presented by the growth study commission say quite a bit about the dimensions of that structure. The analysts really missed something by ignoring it."

Toner provides the following example of an opportunity missed by the authors of Volume V:

The simple fact is that if the residents are well employed and retain a good income [even under some reduced growth alternative], then they would be willing to bear a heavier tax load in exchange for some socially and environmentally responsible form of nongrowth. The authors

mention this general idea several times, but they don't
really dig into the issue.

Toner appears to have found some evidence of academic and
professional timidity on the part of the economic consultant and University of Colorado economics professors who worked on Volume V.
It is difficult to say whether this is the case or whether the Boulder
citizens put too much faith in the local expertise on growth, including
the various contributions from the University of Colorado.

For example, the authors of Volume V dealt with such common
nongrowth items as optimum city size and cost-benefit analysis in a
fairly traditional manner, relying almost exclusively on older and
more established research. No real national survey of other local
studies in these areas was attempted. Perhaps the authors were
simply not aware that more pragmatic, locally oriented research was
going on.

"What I wonder," asked Bill Toner, "is who will this report help?"
Toner added that the economists apparently leaned most heavily toward
the first alternative, the continuation of present trends, because they
felt most comfortable talking in these terms.

I noticed the same lack of spark and creativity in Volume VI on
Legal-Political Aspects. This volume analyzes the legal feasibility
of the four alternatives studied by the commission. Like the economists, the legal consultants feel the most comfortable with the first
alternative, the continuation of the status quo. However, they see no
legal problems with the fourth alternative, the one emphasizing social,
economic, and cultural diversity. When it comes to the population
limitation and environmental amenity preservation models, legal consultants Stephen F. Williams and Donald M. Carmichael from the
University of Colorado take a very conservative stance in their section
of the volume and foresee not only automatic court challenges but general victory for the opposition on a wide range of fronts, ranging from
the loss of the presumed validity enjoyed by governmental zoning
authorities, to defeat on the takings issue, a subject covered elsewhere
in this book.

There also appears to be considerable prejudgment that radical
or even mildly radical antigrowth measures in Boulder will be struck
down as exclusionary. At one point, Carmichael and Williams warn
that "Boulder would do well to avoid action that even appears to
sound like 'Let them eat cake!'"[5] This warning is raised in connection with the population limitation alternative in which Boulder would
meet the Denver Council of Governments' fair-share low-income
housing quota. Carmichael and Williams argue that Boulder would
somehow be retreating from its low-income housing commitments
under this policy "in order to save funds for an exclusive golden

ghetto." Such rhetoric certainly will not be helpful if and when Boulder's growth policies are challenged in court.

In general, the various legal consultants who worked on the volume can be chided for a limited selection of case references and a general lack of understanding of the full implications of such potentially helpful cases as Ramapo. The consultants generally rely on rather conservative interpretations of exclusionary zoning from Pennsylvania and New Jersey and seem to have little understanding of the rather dynamic nature of the law in response to environmental and nongrowth issues around the country. Perhaps it is another case of locally based consultants not having a full appreciation of developments at the local level.

As one reads the consultants' reports, one begins to feel that the citizens of Boulder got what they asked for when they concentrated almost exclusively on local consultants, to the exclusion of their own planning department and the experiences from other growth-challenging communities. They became educated on various aspects of growth and probably managed to educate a number of other citizens in Boulder and the surrounding Boulder County. This was a fine first step and perhaps it was all that could be done at the time. But one must wonder whether the $100,000 could not have been put to better use by obtaining a blend of inputs from locals, including the planners, and also from at least a handful of national experts and observers.

SOME OBSERVATIONS BY THE DIRECTOR OF COMMUNITY DEVELOPMENT

The last person I talked to during my field visit to Boulder in December 1973 was the outgoing director of community development, William Lamont. He was the first person I had talked to about Boulder at the ASPO Detroit conference in April 1972. It seemed like a long time between those two meetings. Now he was on his way to a university teaching job in Denver, and I was between jobs, having left my job with the American Society of Planning Officials in Chicago in October 1973.

I asked Lamont some final questions and noted his answers:
1. Did the Boulder Area Growth Study Commission do its job?
Lamont:

> I question whether the study has come up with what their
> original charge was. We haven't lost our momentum as
> far as the citizens are concerned, but the study doesn't
> really tell us where to go. Do we annex more land or
> don't we? What do we do about housing? What do we do

with the interim growth policies adopted by the city council?

2. How do you feel about the four alternatives studied by the commission?
Lamont:

They really worked on four alternate scenarios which were rather inflexible. With scenarios it is difficult to relate to all the citizen input they got and work in changes which will produce different population figures. It would have been better to develop a matrix and a continuum of numbers related to the interplay between isolated variables such as housing, environment, density, etc.

3. If you had it to do over again, would you push harder for a more direct role for yourself and other planners in the growth study?
Lamont:

I still have mixed emotions. We didn't have time when it all began. There were too many things going on. The city should have maintained more control over the project, especially with regard to the selection and direction of consultants. The original decision to stay at arms length was the wrong judgment. We just didn't think the citizens' efforts were going anywhere.

My advice to other cities involved with this kind of study would be. Don't release it to an ad hoc outside group. We had utilized consultants in the past in Boulder and could have gotten more results with the same money. It was more difficult for a citizens' ad hoc committee to work with consultants. The university people had to learn more about the topic before they did their consultant work.

CONCLUSION

Boulder's growth study did not meet all expectations, and the city appeared to be losing some of its innovative momentum toward the end of 1973. Yet, when viewed in a wider context and when compared to other cities of similar size, Boulder still looks like what it is—a sharp community in a sharp area, with a good reservoir of concerned, involved citizens. Boulder still has an impressive array of growth retarding tools and, pending some complete reversals in the courts, should be able to use them. In our opinion, a visit to Boulder or a reading of some of the local growth study reports would be a valuable first step for any citizen or planning official just getting involved in his or her own local nongrowth debate.

Perhaps Boulder is no longer a Camelot of nongrowth. Perhaps we shouldn't expect Camelots to be of lasting duration. In the United States, we have learned this lesson on the national level; perhaps we should learn it on the local level as well. Initial surges of innovation and emotion soon give way to more extended periods of data collection and nuts and bolts implementation. The more philosophical generalists get frustrated or pushed aside as the technical people move in. Maybe this is the way it has to be.

The simple conclusion is that Boulder is a nice place to live at its present size. It has problems, but one feels a strong sense of community identity among the residents. People around the country are still saying "Boulder did it, why can't we try." Maybe if enough places try, a few other Camelots will emerge.

NOTES

1. League of Women Voters, Land Use in the Boulder Area (Boulder, Colorado: July 1973), p. 14.

2. Earl L. Finkler, Nongrowth as a Planning Alternative (Chicago: American Society of Planning Officials, 1972), pp. 33-39.

3. Ibid., pp. 59-65.

4. Ibid., p. 60.

5. Stephen F. Williams and Donald M. Carmichael, "Legal Issues Relating to Growth Control," in Boulder Area Growth Study Commission, Exploring Options for the Future, Volume VI: Legal-Political Aspects—Economic Incentives and Disincentives, City of Boulder, November 1973, p. 11.

4

ECONOMIC EFFECTS
OF GROWTH CONTROL

Most nongrowth proposals and programs immediately confront the issue of "economic impact" or "fiscal impact." In this chapter we look at the emerging state of the art in municipal cost-revenue and cost-benefit analysis and attempt to determine how much light and insight the numerous studies of this kind are bringing to the growth-nongrowth debate.

The analysis leads us rather far afield from economic analysis, as traditionally conceived, into issues of governmental structure, local politics, and numerous other disciplines. The absence of meaningful analyses in this area may, in fact, be partly explained by the multidisciplinary nature of the pertinent subject matter. Even within the economics profession itself, individual analysts often have trouble moving between different divisions of the discipline. And transferability of knowledge from economics to political science or other seemingly unrelated areas is even more rare. While we do not claim to be experts in all the pertinent disciplines, we do have a good deal of familiarity with most of them, and with the ways in which economic studies are currently prepared and used. Accordingly, we feel it might be helpful to try to trace some interdisciplinary connections that will lead to more meaningful and helpful economic studies.

The problems in this area are multiple and interacting, having to do with such things as data availability, technical sophistication of the analyst, confusion about what can be produced and what can realistically be expected from an economic or fiscal study of the impacts of growth, not to mention a pervasive (but perhaps healthy) confusion and debate about what the relevant indicators are and how they are to be measured.

Planning decisions traditionally have been made with a great concern for how the dollars flow. Yet, at the present time, we do not have a clear idea of how or why most of the dollars generated

43

in the urban growth process flow. Furthermore, firmly grounded statistical analysis could do a great deal to advance the nongrowth proponents' arguments in the courts, where it appears that some of the basic decisions on local jurisdictions' abilities to implement growth policy are going to be made in the near future. The emotional arguments that often prevail in the local government setting will fare less well in the judicial setting of adversary presentation, argument, and counterargument. To meet this challenge, a "great leap forward" in the art of economic and fiscal analysis will be required. At present, it appears that this rapid advance will be difficult to bring about. The economic profession is not focused directly on the urban debate—its concerns are elsewhere, in more clearly bounded and defined areas of the profession. Insights from political science, physical science, and numerous other disciplines are needed to provide truly meaningful analysis, but no coordinating mechanism has yet arisen to integrate these insights and knowledge into a comprehensive framework for meaningful urban economic and fiscal analysis. Progress is being made by fits and starts, on isolated battlefronts. There is, however, no discernible concentrated thrust toward coordinated and effective grappling with the economic and fiscal aspects of the growth management issue.

This chapter outlines some of the reasons for failure and confusion, and suggests some directions that might lead to more meaningful fact-finding and analysis in the future. Economic analysis has become a game that "anyone can play." It is hoped that this chapter will help establish a much needed new "par" for the game and help to bring about a sense of common purpose.

PROBLEMS OF DEFINITION

Debates on the subject of growth management begin to fragment into confusion whenever someone asks the simple question, "Growth of what? What's your indicator?"

Strategies proceed from the definition of the problem. Many strategies are based on the attempt to stop only one form or manifestation of growth or one of its visible symbols—numbers of households or housing units. Communities often find that action against one or another symptom often does not have the desired result of stopping or slowing consequences that are seen to flow from the existence of the indicator. Population may remain the same, but school costs may continue to rise, reflecting increased demands for improved quality of service, increased wage demands of school-system employees, or a district's attempt to catch up with expenditures that had been deferred during periods of rapid growth, when more immediate needs had to be met. (Recent studies in the City of Los Angeles concluded that during the period 1967-70, increases in population accounted for only roughly 10 percent of total increases in school cost per capita, the balance being accounted for by the factors described above, among others.)[1] Population may remain stable; but traffic may increase if car ownership per household continues to increase, as has been the pattern in recent years.

Defining Economic Growth

Although cities' primary concerns are generally with fiscal or "assessed value" calculations, there are other, sometimes more meaningful ways in which payoff to a city can be measured. For example, economic growth can be measured by a city in a number of different ways: indicators could include additions or increases in any of the following areas:

- numbers of jobs
- total salaries and payroll
- value of product generated by local firms
- tax contribution of employers to the city and other public agencies (in the form of property, sales, and other taxes)
- absorption of nonresidential land
- building construction
- net contribution (tax revenues less public costs directly associated with the development in question)
- orientation to export business, as compared to local sales

And if, for example, "number of jobs" is taken as the indicator, the more difficult questions remain: Jobs for whom? New residents, or the existing population? What kinds of jobs? Is the development of the local economy creating jobs of the kind that local residents can hold or be trained to hold, or will the jobs be of the kind that require either in-migration of new employees or transferal by the firms of their existing labor force to the new location? But one must also deal with environmental pollution effects. If the jobs for which local residents are qualified, and those which find local locations most attractive, are those with less than ideal environmental side effects, then at what point shall the trade-offs be made? And what are the costs of leveraging out of the situation in which such trade-offs must be made—creating different "conditions" that will attract different types of employers? How much of this kind of determination can be made at the local level, and how much can only be achieved at the regional or state level? (That is, location criteria or skill levels of the labor force.)

45

Industries and firms vary significantly in their costs and benefits to a given community. There are distinct differences in character between one type of growth and another. There are also differences in impact on the local community, depending on the timing and location of growth.

The costs of growth appear in many different forms and are borne in many different ways. Costs of growth may be classified as direct and indirect, short-term and long-term, one-time or continuing. They are borne, in varying degrees, by the public sector, the private sector, and individual households. The following examples illustrate the diversity and range of types of cost:

- Growth costs when it attracts new residents as employees, while leaving local residents unemployed. In this situation, not only is local unemployment not reduced but, in addition, the new residents place added service and facility demands on municipal budgets.
- Growth costs when employment provided by a firm is unstable, dead-end, or both. There may be temporary benefits; but longer-term costs may be incurred (in terms of human resource underutilization).
- Growth costs when it requires major public investment, either in the form of capital investment required to permit establishment of operations or in the form of public annual operating expenditure requirements.
- Growth costs when it generates pollution that adversely affects either the quality of the physical environment or the quality of life of local residents (the two are usually related, although the different effects may appear at different times).

Thus, in most "real world" situations, those evaluating a potential employer firm will have to evaluate a series of cost-benefit trade-offs, balancing the advantages to the city against the undesirable features associated with the firm's presence. The evaluation will have to consider what are the minimal acceptable levels of such negative factors as:

- added pollution, or other factors reducing quality of the natural environment
- instability in employment patterns
- "dead-end" character of jobs offered
- induced migration of additional population to the city as part of the firm's labor force
- public investment requirements

Further, it must be determined whether or not these factors are consistent with community objectives for continued economic growth and
stability. Thus, there must be parallel strategies to encourage maximum economic productivity and to minimize the costs that are created
in the process.

Fiscal, Payroll, and Consumer "Economics"

To further complicate the problem of definitions, most municipal
analyses deal with at least three different varieties of "economics":
fiscal, payroll, and consumer.

Most municipal analyses address themselves primarily to fiscal
issues—calculations of impacts of different levels of growth on tax
base, tax rates, and demands for the services and facilities that have
traditionally been provided by public jurisdictions. The difficulties
associated with this type of analysis are examined in greater detail
later in this chapter.

As the building industry has become more involved in analyses
of growth impacts, it has shifted the focus of analysis toward examination of "payroll economics"—the impact of growth control strategies,
moratoria, and other construction limitation devices on the continuing
viability of the building industry itself.[2] These analyses speak in
terms of construction jobs lost or payrolls reduced and trace the
implications of construction unemployment for unemployment in other
sectors of the economy—that is, they try to estimate the loss of local
service jobs that would result if construction activity were to be substantially reduced. These analyses seem to imply, in many cases,
that there is an assumed "natural" rate of construction employment
(generally, the level of employment that has been maintained in recent
years) and that downward shifts somehow violate an assumed right
of the local industry to continue at its present level of operation.
Few analyses, either public or private, address the question whether
there is an appropriate level of construction employment (as a per-
centage of total employment) and whether recent levels of construction
employment represent an abnormal overheating of that sector.

A third, and somewhat distinct, form of analysis, the least evident in the recent series of studies, has to do with the impact of growth
control programs on individual consumers—in particular, consumers
of housing and housing-related municipal services. The household's
benefit and cost calculations are different in character from those of
either the building industry or any individual municipal government.
There is no question that increased costs of development are in many
cases passed on to the consumer, escalating the price that must be
paid for housing and limiting the numbers of households that can

effectively bid in the market for new housing. Furthermore, the total costs of housing and housing-related services are paid for by consumers through a number of small, and often undocumented, payments to local, state, and federal governments. Few analyses go further than to trace the most visible payments to local agencies (in many cases they do not even consider all the local agencies).

Thus, we have a series of different types of calculations; we have estimations of cost and benefit from the points of view of different "audiences" and involving different types of measurement criteria. Study findings often blur the distinctions between the three types of calculations; this results in a lack of clarity and minimizes the usefulness of analytical results.

The "Comprehensive" Approach

If the attempt to zero in on one indicator or one type of growth has been unsuccessful, so have most of the efforts to arrive at a comprehensive solution that takes into account all the interacting and impinging factors. In most metropolitan areas or communities there are little or no data on many of the most important variables in the equation. Even if detailed data were available there would be serious problems of cross-comparability. Comparisons of income levels, population levels, and pollution levels, presented in various quantitative formats, quickly become confusing and meaningless. In such a context, one has to choose between overdocumentation, knowing that the use of the information will be descriptive rather than analytical, and oversimplification through the use of "common denominators," which often results in an attempt to compare items that are, for all practical purposes, not comparable.

Many of the advantages that are thought to be derived from policies and programs of nongrowth represent qualitative items and value judgments—a "unique community" or "preservation of local character." While attempts are made to quantify the unquantifiable, they more often confuse than clarify. "Optimal quality" for residents of one neighborhood may be something entirely different from "optimal quality" for residents of another.

Value judgments again enter the picture when considerations of "par" must be raised and incorporated. Is the present income distribution of a given community "optimal?" Perhaps it is optimal for the community as a whole, compared with other communities, but perhaps not for those individuals who comprise the bottom half or two-thirds of the distribution. Recognition of this difference in perceptions leads to consideration of distributive solutions, of a social planning nature, that are far removed from the traditional purview of the land use planner. It is coming to be recognized that equity and distribution issues are often relatively independent of a community's or a region's posture on the growth versus nongrowth issue. Changes in the current distribution of incomes must be brought about through changes in distribution mechanisms that operate independently, for the most part, of the mechanisms that govern rates of growth.

ECONOMIC ANALYSIS RELATED TO GROWTH MANAGEMENT EFFORTS

A number of studies and analyses dealing with various aspects of the economic impact of growth control and growth management strategies are under way or have recently been completed. We can make some general comments and draw some general conclusions about the present state of the art in economic analysis of this subject matter.

First, as is the case with "growth" subject matter in general, much of the argument and debate concerns the question of what it is relevant or important to measure. In the area of economic and fiscal analysis, these questions include:

- For what universe (local or regional)?
- Over what period of time (long range or short range)?
- With what attempt to quantify qualitative variables?
- Under what assumptions (as, for example, regarding efficiencies or diseconomies thought to be achieved through increased scale)?

Much of the problem with the use of economic analyses stems from the fact that they are often commissioned in an attempt to find clear, clean answers to such questions as "Will this be profitable to the community or not? By how much?" The simple fact is that the subject matter under consideration does not lend itself to this type of answer (although some economic analysts confuse the picture by writing their reports as though such clear answers were possible). This mystique of certainty represents an unfortunate transposition of economic analysis as used in the business and real estate development setting, where concepts of return, payout, and bottom line have direct applicability, to the urban development and municipal finance arena, where such items as externalities, transfer payments, and threshold considerations cloud the issue.

The answer to "better or worse" questions in the urban setting is further complicated by the "compared to what" question. In terms of its own fiscal well-being, an individual city may be "better off" in the short term by choosing a nongrowth policy; but the city may be contributing to and encouraging a regional pattern of settlement and job location that is inefficient, or less efficient than an alternate regional pattern in which individual local governments are given less freedom to place restrictions on development. The inefficiencies may show up in the form of weakened economic strength of the region or in the form of social costs in other areas of the region (for example, costs of ghetto containment), which may or may not show up as costs to the suburban resident.

Two forms of education appear to be called for. First, those who conduct analyses should be made aware of the range of issues that should be considered, the importance of bounding the analysis in time and space and of stating appropriate limits and qualifications, the need for acceptance and statement of the uncertainties and unpredictables, and possible influence of these uncertainties on the findings of a given analysis.

Second, those who commission and rely upon such analyses should be made aware of the appropriate limits of reliance on the analyses, the point at which the usefulness of economic information declines and political judgment takes over, the need for acceptance of the uncertainties inherent in this type of analysis, and the reasons for these uncertainties. In other words, both analyst and client should become increasingly aware that the primary purpose of economic and fiscal analyses is to provide an understanding of relationships between actions and consequences and to provide a clearer understanding of what causes what (and in what degree) rather than to provide definitive answers or "final numbers."

The studies conducted to date seem to indicate the existence of an "excluded middle." Studies tend to be either too simple or overdocumented. Although examples of simplistic analysis abound, a far more serious problem, one that involves far greater waste, is represented by the numerous analyses and reports that err on the side of providing a great quantity of information rather than an explanation of its relevance, reports that hide weak assumptions and methodology behind a blizzard of statistics and equations. These analyses of the "overkill" variety are damaging in three respects. First, they represent a massive waste of human and computer time, not to mention money. Second, they divert the reader from consideration of real issues and significant relationships and impart an unwarranted aura of magic to the proceedings, often leading decision makers to defer overmuch to the conclusions and recommendations of the technical adviser. Finally, such analyses tempt decision makers to hide behind a continuing program of study as a means of avoiding rather than confronting issues that sooner or later, probably far later, will be seen not to be solvable with economic analysis techniques after all.

As a general rule, the closer an economic analysis stays to the ground and the more limited the arena of analysis and closely defined the subject matter, the more helpful and accurate it is likely to be. For example, economic analyses are an absolute necessity in the bargaining process that surrounds negotiation over densities and related matters in planned unit development. Here the trade-offs are relatively clear and finite, the time horizons often short term, and investments, both public and private, well bounded. Yet there is a great deal of room for refinement of analysis even in this simple area. A recent study of cost-benefit analysis in the Planned-Unit Development (PUD) setting[3] illustrates that even at the simplest level there are areas where educated guesses are in order and where decisions must be made on the basis of incomplete information.

At the citywide or regional level, complications in the analysis increase at least geometrically as land area, number of jurisdictions, and numbers of persons increase arithmetically. Thus, while the rationale for increased generalization and qualifying statements is dramatically increased, few analysts hedge their bets in realistic qualifying language.

The fault lies on both sides. Some economists and economic analysts have been so trained, often in areas of the profession other than urban economics, that they resist qualified answers, feeling that professional integrity or reputation demands a firm and final answer, backed by rigorous analysis and methodology. In the urban setting, however, this search for certainty is often counterproductive, resulting in the "drunk under the lamp post mistake" (the drunk looked for his keys under the lamp post because the light was better there). The analyst chooses the most quantifiable area—the area in which the best and most detailed data are available—and proceeds to conclusions based on that data, often with minimal regard for the relevance of those particular data in the overall context.

Misdirection or misuse of study findings by clients is an equally severe problem. Clients sometimes ask the wrong question, innocently or otherwise. For example, a client may ask the analyst to evaluate the impact of a development on the basis of only a few criteria. The analyst proceeds as instructed and brings back the answer, failing to add that the answer might have been different if other factors had been considered. The limited finding is then, in many cases, touted and used for broader purposes of justification, sometimes without malice aforethought, sometimes with. Client and analyst alike feel more comfortable with positive, clean answers. They commission studies and analyze data in the hope of reaching such answers. The dice may be consciously or unconsciously loaded in that direction. One development organization in California commissioned a study of the municipal impact of a proposed development, specifically directing that school costs be excluded from the calculation. Consultants who pointed out that these costs should be included for a meaningful analysis were dropped from further consideration by the client.

There is now a growing pile of statistical information stored in computers, in files, and in the planning offices of urban and suburban America. In a mass exercise of professional uncertainty, more is being piled up before analysts gird themselves for the more important task of actually applying the information to the analysis and solution of development-related problems. The justification usually given is the need for comprehensiveness and full visibility before "running the model." As the piles of information, and the costs of maintaining them mount, a massive credibility gap is interposing itself between those who hold out the promise of answers through economic analysis and those who are waiting for those answers. It seems that we run a very real risk of a major backlash of sentiment on the part of local decision makers; they may shift from a feeling that "data will save us" to a knee-jerk counterreaction that "data is no damn use at all." For everybody's sake, some admissions should be made, some tentative steps taken toward reality by both sides, in the interest of more informed decision making.

The rather primitive state of the art of economic and fiscal analysis as applied to the urban setting is acknowledged by many of its practitioners.[4] They point out that urban economics as currently practiced is not a coherent discipline within the field of economics but draws from numerous areas of economic thinking, providing insights that are sometimes cumulative and synergistic, but sometimes contradictory to one another. Also, issues of political science and public administration, to name just two of the most common related fields, impinge upon and often dictate or strongly influence the results of many studies that are nominally "economic." Compounding the confusion is that even if consultants and economic analysts are beginning to ask the right questions, clients are often not. Although it is generally coming to be recognized that the region or metropolitan area is the appropriate framework for analysis of the issues, few of the clients commissioning studies represent regional interests. Most of the studies being done deal with, and are responsive to the concerns of, local government rather than regional government.

The consulting profession considers itself to be partly responsible for this state of affairs. Many analysts continue to undertake assignments that involve answering the wrong question for the wrong client, feeling that the wrong or suboptimal client may well be the only client in town, and that there is something to be gained by at least shedding the maximum possible light on that client's problem, even if the arena for analysis is not ideal. However, these analysts often hide qualifications to conclusions in appendixes or footnotes in such a way that the tightness of the constraints to analysis, or the limited applicability of a given analysis, is often not as clearly presented as it might be.

THE FISCAL ANALYST'S DILEMMA

In order to accurately analyze the profitability of a given development, it is necessary to identify the existing fiscal network, outlining the revenue and cost flows by function and by governmental level (federal, state, county, local, and intermetropolitan). It is unrealistic, however, to assume that the current balance of governmental responsibility will be maintained in the future. It is also virtually impossible to predict the ways in which these responsibilities will be shifted, other than to say that the balance is likely to undergo significant change. Changes in federal or state assumption of responsibility for a given function (for example, welfare, health, education, or housing) can and have altered municipal profiles in significant ways. Thus, any analysis must be regarded as a snapshot of the fiscal profile at one point in time; the usefulness of the analysis as a vehicle for predicting the future decreases the farther into the future projections are made.

For example, few studies analyze the total burden (federal, state, and local) on the local resident. Most studies restrict themselves to calculation of the largest and most visible impacts—the property tax impacts at the local level. It is, of course, difficult to trace the incremental addition of cost to the suburban resident of increasing compaction of the ghetto that lies beyond his jurisdiction, of increasing air pollution and the required corrective expenditures, and of added regional water pollution and sewage treatment facilities. The relationship between any one development and increases in these less visible, more broadly distributed costs is so far from obvious that few have attempted to trace and quantify it.

Most local suburban attempts to provide a fiscal justification for growth limitation look reasonable on paper because many of the costs of exclusion appear in the form of externalities—decreases in the quality of somebody else's environment. The people who end up paying these costs cannot trace them to the jurisdiction of their origin. Furthermore, the costs to the affected jurisdiction are the result of a series of causal effects generated by a number of jurisdictions with similar policies. The pain caused by the white noose of exclusionary suburbs comes not from any one strand, but from the effect of all strands pulling together. Effect from any one requires the presence of all. But documentation of the incidence of these externalities is a difficult process at best.

The City as a Profit-Maximizing Corporation

Although the point seems obvious in retrospect, analysts are
only now beginning to recognize that it makes no more sense to generalize about a group of public municipal corporations (cities) than
it does to generalize about a group of private corporations. Each
has its own peculiar and unique asset base, set of revenue and cost
streams, profit motivations (ranging from aggressively profit-oriented
to custodial, maintenance-oriented), and investment strategy. Some
cities, for example, have attempted to leverage their assets through
use of federal funds and by exercising their bonding power to permissible limits, while others have adopted a closer-to-the-vest "pay as
you go" policy, maintaining program levels supportable by year-to-
year tax rates (not including bonded indebtedness) found to be acceptable to their electorates.

There is, of course, one significant difference between the public
and the private corporation, and it complicates any analysis of the
profitability of a given development or development policy. Municipal
corporations, as a general rule, cannot go bankrupt (with certain
possible exceptions such as Newark, New Jersey, which is reportedly
teetering on the edge of insolvency, and state takeover of functions).
The expenditure resulting from added growth can, as a general rule,
be offset in any given year by increases in the local property tax
rate to achieve the balanced budget required by law. And so, in the
case of municipal fiscal analysis, the question less often concerns
what can legally be done to respond to costs of growth than what the
electorate will politically permit to be done, and against what standards. In far too many cities, the standard for what can and should
be done in terms of public expenditure levels turns out to be "last
year's tax rate." In many cities the maintenance of a stable tax rate
is the most sacred of municipal sacred cows. Councils that increase
tax rates and city managers who recommend increases are, as a
general rule, quite vulnerable politically.

Unfortunately, this visible symbol of increased cost is more
meaningful to the electorate than the more subtle, usually hidden
costs that appear in the form of gradual declines in quality or levels
of service. In the late 1960s, an era of pervasive public sector wage
and salary demands and inflationary increases in material and equip-
ment costs, stable tax rates and assessed valuation figures often
meant declining levels of service over the years or gradual shifts
of portions of the budget from less visible maintenance and house-
keeping functions to more visible annual payroll accounts. The result
has been a maintenance of quality in the face of increasing costs in
the most visible areas of public service provision, and a slow deterioration of quality and level of maintenance in the less visible areas.

Many cities now find themselves with increasing backlogs of maintenance needs in such areas as street maintenance—and a program of brush-fire response to emergencies where the problems become visible, in isolated instances.

This problem of having to run hard in order to stay in the same place is particularly intense in those cities which control only a small portion of the expenditure decisions that make up the total tax rate. In most California cities, for example, the city tax rate accounts for only about $1 to $2 of an average $11 to $12 combined tax rate—a combined rate that may include the levies of 15 or more jurisdictions. Levies of independent school districts, which are not necessarily (nor often) coterminous with cities, generally account for $5 to $6 of the combined rate. Thus, pressure for increased expenditure in any major jurisdiction requires counter pressures downward on the part of others if the combined rate is to be maintained at an acceptable level. Local (city) officials, being at the most visible points in the system, most often bear the brunt of voter dissatisfaction with increases in the combined rate, even if these increases result from actions of other, less accountable actors elsewhere in the system.

Classification of Studies by Type

Economic and fiscal analyses dealing with the impacts of growth take a number of different forms—some of them specific and limited, others more cosmic and generalized. We conclude the chapter with a brief description of these different types of analyses, and attempt to predict which areas of study are likely to yield valuable insights in the future.

Cost-Revenue Studies

Cost-revenue studies are, as the name implies, most often pure comparisons of dollars against dollars. As such they restrict themselves to the most visible revenue and expenditure figures and come closest to traditional municipal accounting. In their concentration on accurate tracing of costs to and revenues of the municipality, such studies more often than not provide a misleading illusion of accuracy. They tend to overlook some of the more pertinent impacts of a given development or development pattern, since many of these impacts are not very susceptible to the type of quantification needed for such a balance sheet approach. Such an approach is most useful for analysis of smaller developments where the short-term trade-offs are likely to be more obvious, as in the case of city-developer negotiations on sewer extensions to serve a 5-acre subdivision.

55

Cost-Benefit Analysis

Cost-benefit studies throw (or attempt to throw) a broader conceptual or geographic net over the range of externalities generated by a given development or development pattern. Such studies tend not only to be broader in scope but to deal with a longer time span than the cost-revenue study. Much of the confusion surrounding economic studies on the subject of growth control and policy stems from the blurring of definitions between cost-revenue and cost-benefit studies. Analysts with more of a cost-revenue orientation deal with quantifiable items, extending their focus outward to those cost and revenue indicators that can be statistically traced over an area larger than the city in question. They remain, however, tied to a basic municipal accounting framework.

Analysts at the other end of the spectrum seek to bring either marginally quantifiable or unquantifiable factors into the equation (on the cost or benefit side, depending on the orientation of the analyst or client). Among the factors they consider are the following:

- Costs of containment of central city population, municipal overburden in the central city, resulting from "white noose" suburban exclusion policies
- Benefits of "local self-determination," open space, higher quality of life, expanded residential choice (unique suburban communities versus homogenized blandness)
- Incremental contributions to various forms of environmental deterioration

Many of the most lively debates in the area of growth control are over the appropriate range and coverage of such studies. As quantifiability declines, value judgments enter the void and debates ensue between those who feel that a high quality of life means a five-acre farm and those who prefer the intense interaction of the high density community.

The cost-benefit analysis is most appropriate at the regional or metropolitan level—the level at which most relevant externalities can be captured and accounted for. As we have noted, however, few metropolitan areas have advanced politically to the point where there are clients to commission such studies, and fewer yet to the point where there are sufficient data available to provide meaningful results in a study of this type. In this kind of situation, intentions are generally good but very difficult to implement.

It is perhaps significant to note that cost-benefit studies had their initiation, and most intensive use, in areas such as water resources management, where the full range of pertinent variables (crop values, savings of losses from flood control, user benefits of recreationists) was more easily quantified. Translation of this analytical framework from the rural setting of water resources management has been difficult; the urban setting, with its intricacies and interdependencies, has proved to be a far more intractable analytical beast.

OPTIMAL CITY SIZE AND SPECIFIC MUNICIPAL FUNCTIONS

Analyses of optimal city size have been with us since at least the time of Plato. Like the most far-reaching of cost-benefit analyses, they run the risk of neglecting quantitative detail and placing too much emphasis on conclusions that, more closely examined, turn out to be thinly veiled statistical rationalizations of preconceived value judgments. Comparisons of one city to another, or of various cities of the same or different populations, have generally made the mistake of assuming a uniformity of corporate function, style, and purpose among all municipal corporations.

As analysts of "optimal size" come to recognize the complex economic forces operating behind population numbers, and effects of these forces on the nature and function of cities, optimal size studies are becoming increasingly useful. The search for specificity is leading analysts from cosmic generalization to detailed considerations of the costs of individual municipal government activities and the factors that influence such costs.

Studies of specific municipal functional areas—such as police service, fire protection, education, and municipal management— represent a slowly moving but latently powerful component of the overall analysis of the impacts of growth. They are the logical response to general dissatisfaction with the generality of the "optimal city size" studies. They delve more deeply, and more carefully, into the components that combine to make up the total profile of municipal cost that eventually becomes visible to the all-important municipal electorate.

It has been traditional in American society for those decisions affecting most basic human needs, and those least visible to the public, to be delegated furthest afield. Metropolitan southern California gets its water from 300 miles away and more, through the good offices of state and federal water projects. The sewage treatment for over 100 independent communities in the Los Angeles basin is handled by the massive Hyperion plant, through which millions of gallons of sewage pass each day. Telephone service to a combined total of over 10 million persons is provided by two public utilities regulated by the state Public Utilities Commission, and there are relatively few complaints from local jurisdictions regarding the lack of local control over these functions. In each case, it is regarded as rather inevitable that this is the way things should be, since this is the way things have been.

And yet, within the same metropolitan area, cities stuggle fiercely to maintain their independence and individual decision-making power when the decisions to be made have to do with who shall live next door and who shall have the responsibility for deciding how much profit should be made from the use of a given parcel of land.

The problem, in other words, apparently has to do with how impacts of a given decision are perceived. Do they affect the individual primarily, and others secondarily? And what is the ratio of primary to secondary? How much does a given decision impinge on the individual's "quality of life" or ability to make money—and how much and how on others'? The location of decision-making power for a given function appears to be a function of the electorate's perception of the immediacy and intensity of localized as against more broadly distributed consequences.

If the governmental structure is the result of the sum total of perceptions and attitudes, it may be argued that any data input that alters these perceptions and attitudes eventually serves to bring about a more rational public decision calculus regarding the inter-related questions of how much to spend for performance of a given governmental function and the appropriate place for the spending to take place.

Specific function studies and analyses perform just that function. They are, as a rule, less successful in making suburban jurisdictions aware of the externality-generating consequences of their policies than they are in giving the more impacted jurisdictions—central cities, in particular—the ammunition they ne⌒ to take effective positions in regional forums and to debate, from some statistical base, the steadily increasing torrent of externally-generated cost that threatens to erode their vitality.

It is one of the ironies of present-day metropolitan America that the cities which most need to defend themselves against increasing costs of growth, the older central cities, are generally the least equipped to do so. Although some defense of the central city position is beginning to emerge from academic sources,[5] there has been a lack of response from the central city jurisdictions themselves, with some notable exceptions. (For example, the public statements of Mayor Henry Maier of Milwaukee urging nongrowth or possibly negative growth for that city, apparently adopting the Forrester Urban Dynamics theories regarding the degenerative negative feedback loop brought into play by present central city policies; the positions taken by James Banks, District of Columbia housing officer, and Melvin Mister, executive director of the Redevelopment Land Agency of the District of Columbia, proposing cessation of low-income and moderate-income housing development in the District until such time as regional policies for dispersal of units had been developed regionwide—proposing, in the case of Banks, to use legal procedures for the eviction of tenants who were delinquent in their rent payments in public housing in the District, contrary to the more humane, though perhaps extralegal forbearance procedures that had been employed by the D.C. Housing Authority in recent years.)

On closer examination, the unresponsiveness of most central city jurisdictions is perhaps not surprising. Central city governments, as a general rule, demonstrate the characteristics of the "mature organization" with a vengeance. In many, authority have become fragmented over the years as the result of a series of good government charter amendments, each designed to block abuses of the moment, but resulting, in cumulative process, in a system that does very little but does it in carefully documented detail and with massive scrutiny. What legal authority exists is often exercised, or more often not exercised, by long-tenure civil servants who value career security more than aggressive action. And even in those few cities where powers and personalities combine in an effective action-oriented government, these powers and talents are more often used in fighting the day-to-day battles for municipal survival and avoidance of total system breakdown than in dealing with the more abstract, longer-term issues of regional responsibility and relationships.

Viewed against this setting, in which those who have the most to lose by continuance of the present system have the least power and those who have the most to gain (at least in the short term) by its preservation have the most power, the clearing of the air with step-by-step analyses of who is paying how much for what comes as a rather refreshing and helpful and optimistic indication of the possibility of gradual change.

If nothing else, such studies offer helpful advice to the suburban city manager in his attempt to fight off the squeeze that, unless resisted, erodes quality of service provision, possibly even in an environment of nongrowth. The studies offer ammunition to those at state and regional levels who seek to rationalize the governmental structure for service provision in the interest of greater efficiency and lowered costs. Finally, they help to expose to public view and debate the all-important questions of where the externalities fall, where they come to ground, and with what consequences.

The process of exposure and education is slow. Police analysts speak a different language from water analysts or education analysts. Generalizations are seldom possible from one metropolitan area to another. Nevertheless, the data are being collected, SMSA by SMSA, across the nation. They feed into a strong American concern for having things done more efficiently and more effectively. The consolidators of this information are, for the most part, invisible—a city manager here, a city council there. But the buildup of information is taking place; changes are being made. If studies of this type can fill the void, can bring about a more reasoned discourse on the subject of municipal costs—where they fall, and who bears them—the result is likely to be a positive contribution to the overall attempt to achieve rationally managed growth on a region-by-region and city-by-city basis.

These analyses of municipal cost by function serve, perhaps most importantly, to raise the debate above local (and often petty) considerations and arguments, and to turn it toward consideration of regional trade-offs, costs and benefits. For, as many analysts point out, many of the issues of government cost are, when more closely probed, issues of government structure and of responsibility for specific functions. Added visibility of this fact focuses the spotlight of analysis and reform increasingly on the subject matter where real progress and real breakthroughs are likely to be made.

NOTES

1. City of Los Angeles Planning Department, City of Los Angeles: Needs-Revenue Study, 1972.
2. See, for example, San Diego Construction Industries Coordinating Council, The Copley Report (San Diego: 1974).
3. R. L. Crouch and R. E. Weintraub, "Planned Unit Development: Cost-Benefit Analysis," Urban Land (June 1973): 4.
4. See, for example, Werner Hirsch, Urban Economic Analysis (New York: McGraw-Hill, 1974); and remarks of Philip G. Hammer (Hammer, Siler, George Associates), at the Urban Research Corporation "Managed Growth" Conference, September 1973.
5. See, for example, Wilbur Steger, "Economic and Social Costs of Residential Segregation," in Modernizing Urban Land Policy, Marion Clawson, ed. (Baltimore: Johns Hopkins Press, 1973); and Eric J. Branfman, Benjamin I. Cohen, and David M. Trubek, "Measuring the Invisible Wall: Land Use Controls and Residential Patterns of the Poor," Yale Law Journal 82, (1973): 482.

5

NONGROWTH AND THE
PLANNING PROFESSION

In this chapter we examine the past, present, and probable future reaction of the planning profession and other possible actors to the emerging "new mood" of nongrowth sentiment. As the initial portion of the chapter suggests, many planners were caught off balance by the recent shift in public sentiment and by the nature of the public demands being made on the planning process. In most planning departments, confusion still reigns supreme; planners paw the earth at the fork in the road, searching for signals that will indicate whether nongrowth is a sentiment with staying power, or merely a short-term aberration and fad, to be humored but not to be responded to with any basic reorientations in the planning process.

Next we explore some of the reasons why we feel the profession was caught by surprise, and why we think it is likely that it will continue to be only minimally responsive to demands for basic change. Finally, we examine some alternatives to the present system, pointing out how the identified planning gap may be filled by people who are not "planners" as traditionally conceived; we include some thoughts on a whole new nongrowth profession. As the discussion indicates, some of these alternatives are being put into practice, and we can expect to see more of this in the future. It has been argued by some that planning is too important to be left to planners. It appears that in many jurisdictions, planning is in fact being done by many persons other than planners, although it is too early to tell whether this represents a positive or negative development. However we judge them, the shifts in roles and functions appear to be bringing about some basic changes in the operation of municipal government—changes that could hold the promise of more effective regulation and management of growth.

The personal sections of this chapter were prepared by Earl Finkler.

NONGROWTH TAKES THE PLANNING
PROFESSION BY SURPRISE

Those working as city, regional, and state planners, whose job it is to cast a trained eye on the future, were generally caught by surprise when the movement we now know as nongrowth emerged in the early 1970s in a number of scattered communities across the nation. Kevin Lynch and other planning authorities have noted that planning is really the management of change. At that time, planners were busy trying to manage, mostly in a reactive manner, too much social, physical, and economic change. They were also trying to tell everyone what a great job they were doing and how much planning budgets should be increased to continue this good work.

Toward the end of the 1960s, as the environmentalists and others started their "greening of America," and as more and more suburbs suffered growing pains, people started to doubt that growth was being properly managed. To use a baseball analogy, managers are given pay raises and long-term contracts only when they are shown to be consistent winners.

Nongrowth seems to threaten planners in some very special ways. It is only human for them to avoid it or push it away. The planning profession is particularly vulnerable, being both relatively new and relatively unscientific, especially in the United States.

Perhaps the best way to show how nongrowth surprised planners is to note the rather uneven response of the two large national planning organizations. The first is the American Society of Planning Officials (ASPO) in Chicago. ASPO is primarily a service organization to some 10,000 planners and 1,200 planning agencies in the United States and Canada. In the past few years ASPO has also started a rather massive sponsored research program, charting and analyzing new trends and techniques in land use, and this should give the organization more resources and manpower to respond to nongrowth. But aside from the two planning advisory service reports I prepared while working for ASPO in 1972 and 1973, the organization has done little to stimulate and coordinate local nongrowth actions.

The second is the more "professional" planning organization, the American Institute of Planners (AIP), headquartered in Washington, D.C. AIP has about 7,000 members, but at the end of 1973, as far as we could determine, it did not have sufficient recorded response to the nongrowth movement to justify analysis.

One incident typifies the early response of planning organizations to nongrowth. In the summer of 1971, William Lamont, the director of community development for Boulder, Colorado, sent AIP headquarters a well-written descriptive article on his community's pioneering growth-challenging efforts. AIP turned down his article

62

for publication, reportedly because it felt that "there was not enough interest in this topic across the nation."

The theme of the 1971 ASPO National Planning Conference, held in New Orleans from March 27 to April 1, was, interestingly enough, "The Making of a National Urban Growth Policy," but the word "nongrowth" did not appear anywhere in the conference program or in the various speeches. The term did appear in a major precon-ference article I wrote on New Orleans, as the conference location, for the ASPO newsletter:

> In some ways, New Orleans is also a poor location for a conference on "Making National Growth Policy," espe-cially if growth is viewed in traditional terms. A topic with more local relevance would be a national urban non-growth policy or, as Dean John Lawrence of Tulane's School of Architecture puts it, a policy of "civilized decay."
>
> "Civilized decay" should not be confused with "benign neglect" or other calls to inaction. Dean Lawrence noted that New Orleans is already in the process of decay, but that this decay is "unplanned and ungoverned." "What is needed is a real dedication to quality, something that is often missing here," he said, adding that the city shouldn't use such cities as Dallas, Atlanta, and Houston as models, but should instead work out its own unique place in 20th century America. "We should first make the city livable for its residents—then the tourists will come," he said.[1]

Shortly after the ASPO conference, Dean Lawrence died and so did some of this fine man's innovative ideas. Today, New Orleans is more famous for its new domed stadium than for any real policy of nongrowth and civilized decay.

The 1972 ASPO National Planning Conference was held in Detroit from April 15 to 20. Its theme was "The Urban Fringe and the Urban Core." Once again, there was nothing about nongrowth on the formal program, despite the fact that several ASPO staff members had suggested such a session. In addition, several planners in local agencies around the nation wrote to ASPO requesting a nongrowth session. But the Society's conference planners held firm in their decision not to devote a formal session to nongrowth.

I decided to set up an ad hoc nongrowth session in Detroit and circulated a few notices around the massive expanse of Cobe Hall. The chairmen of a few of the scheduled sessions were asked to announce the ad hoc session. A few made the announcement in a humorous tone, while others reportedly made some passing comment to the idea that nongrowth is just a new form of exclusionary zoning.

Despite the lack of publicity and the fact that the ad hoc session was held during the dinner hour, nearly 150 conference attendees showed up. The session began with a process now quite familiar to nongrowth conference participants—the scrambled exchange of documents, information, and bibliographic notes. I had ordered 20 copies of the now-famous Club of Rome study, The Limits to Growth.[2] These sold out in a few minutes. There were also free summary handouts from the U.S. Commission on Population Growth and the American Future. Several planners from the nearby community of Ann Arbor handed out summaries of their growth study project and many people jotted down titles and contacts as they crowded around the podium. It took perhaps 20 to 25 minutes to begin the more formal discussion in this very informal session. Theodore Kreines, a planning consultant from Connecticut, had written to me before the Detroit conference and offered to participate in any kind of session on nongrowth. As it turned out, we acted a cochairmen. I used a blackboard to show some of the doomsday graphs from the Club of Rome report and Kreines gave a short talk about the impact of nongrowth policies on central cities, suburbs, and exurban areas. These were the only prepared remarks and the group spent the next hour and a half listening to anyone who wanted to take the floor; we ended up discussing the various issues all around the room.

Those attending the ad hoc session were invited to write down their names and addresses. This initial list of some 35 people from various parts of the country served as a general mailing list as my research on nongrowth continued. Everyone on the list was provided with a copy of the master list. Some people used it to distribute their own information or request material from various sources. At the end of the conference, ASPO circulated a questionnaire asking attendees to rate the most popular sessions. The ad hoc nongrowth session ranked high.

THE NONGROWTH STRUGGLE FOR PLANNERS' RESPECT

Not all the action on nongrowth was confined to planners' conferences, although the conferences have been nearly saturated by the topic. The real action continued to take place in such communities as Boulder, Colorado, and Orange County, California. Yet the planners out in the field who felt that nongrowth was a rapidly emerging topic worthy of serious concern by the planning profession had to struggle for recognition or even exposure.

In August 1971, William Lamont sent a longer version of his article on the Boulder, Colorado, nongrowth situation to the American

Society of Planning Officials (ASPO) in Chicago. "I sent it to them for publication or distribution because we were starting to get so many requests for information from all around the country," Lamont said. "I thought ASPO could help me get the word out," he added. Lamont was possibly also looking for a little support from the largest planning organization in the country. He opened the article in rather strong terms:

> Many communities, and their respective states, are presently in the throes of setting policies to discourage growth, limit growth, or more dramatically, stop growth. For the first time in this country, we are questioning the long-accepted proposition that a community must grow to live, and that a community which does not grow is not progressive.
>   . . . Can growth be limited, can it be done in a systematic manner, and can it be done on a basis that does not foster discrimination on the basis of income or race? I think so. The issue is no longer a question of "can we" or "should we," but rather a realization that, if planning is to be meaningful, we are obligated to establish optimum city sizes and then plan for population distribution around the larger metropolitan areas based on these optimum sizes.[3]

Lamont's paper was not published or distributed by ASPO, although there did not seem to be any conscious attempt made to suppress it. A black planner on the ASPO staff was assigned to read it; he concluded that Boulder was trying to push some exclusionary policies. He noted, for example, a statement in the paper that Boulder intended to encourage more subsidized housing, but apparently only for people already employed in the community. Planners are right to thoroughly consider the possible exclusionary aspects of nongrowth, but too often, it seems, such consideration ends their inquiry into this vital topic. There are some serious exclusionary implications in nongrowth, but there are also some considerations such as redistribution of resources, energy conservation, and a resistance to rapid change that make the idea well worth much more intellectual and professional inquiry.

Toward the end of 1971, however, ASPO kept receiving more and more reports from communities engaged in nongrowth debates. A number of these were in response to a notice I placed in TAB, the Society's job bulletin. The notice, repeated several times in November and December, started off by noting that "nongrowth is a popular topic of conversation, but perhaps a less popular or less understood concept in terms of general planning statements and strategies. ASPO is undertaking a study of nongrowth in planning terms."

65

The TAB notices and several short articles and requests for information published in the ASPO newsletter Planning resulted in a number of written and telephone responses by the end of 1971 and in early 1972. A few spontaneous reports on local nongrowth activity filtered in to the ASPO office at about the same time.

THE PLANNING DEPARTMENT OF
ORANGE COUNTY, CALIFORNIA

One of the earliest and most informative responses came from the Orange County, California, planning department. In a letter sent to me in early January 1972, Planning Director Forest Dickason wrote:

> We are involved in an effort . . . aimed at finding out
> whether growth can and should be influenced locally and,
> if so, toward what ends. However, in response to the
> request of the recent ASPO Newsletter, we are enclosing
> four documents which may be of some interest to your
> research. All of these are related to an 11 month study
> which is currently underway and is entitled, "Orange
> County, California Population Growth Policy and Develop-
> ment Strategy Program." Briefly, the purpose of this
> program is twofold: (1) To define both the positive and
> negative aspects of the relationship between population
> growth and environmental quality; and (2) To identify the
> nature and range of the choices which local government
> can make to affect a consciously articulated "Population
> Growth Policy and Development Strategy" for Orange
> County, California. It should be noted that prior to the
> past few years, most citizens were inclined to accept
> population growth, regardless of the less obvious conse-
> quences, as a necessary correlate to economic well-being.
> This program goes far beyond that limited perspective to
> identify the relationship between population growth and
> environmental quality in the broadest sense of the term.

Dickason's letter and the subsequent cooperation of staff planners Albert Bell and William Toner led directly to the inclusion of Orange County as one of the three areas I visited in April and May 1972 to do case studies for the ASPO report on nongrowth.[4] The concern expressed in Dickason's letter regarding the "nature and range of choices" local government can make relative to population growth and development has emerged as one of the basic nongrowth issues. By the end of 1973, there were still no easy answers to the question of the appropriate governmental level at which to regulate growth, although the local governments (cities and counties) have a good lead in this area and should be encouraged to continue any and all responsible activity.

THE PLANNING REPORT OF WAYNE
COUNTY, MICHIGAN

Most of the nongrowth mail ASPO received was from the West, with the East coast not too far behind. But one of the best of the early reports came from Wayne County, Michigan (Detroit and surrounding area). This comprehensive planning report, received by ASPO in June 1971, started off by noting:

> From many quarters, we receive warnings of future crises in ecological matters. This report seeks to recognize the seriousness of some of these issues and, without pushing the panic button, offer programs that will use the lead time that is available before the irreversible crisis stage is reached to prevent that stage from being reached.[5]

It is interesting to see planners using the term "lead time" followed by a warning of possible "irreversible crises" that might take place if such time is not used wisely. Before the environmental movement took hold, planners were not in the habit of thinking this way. Nothing seemed to be irreversible, and if the first amount of lead time was not used properly, a new time frame and work program could be devised, along with a new and larger budget. Some of the recommendations in the Wayne County report were also ahead of their time, including the following:

A. Establish an optimum population range for the County, so that the total spatial needs of the population can be met.
B. Adopt policies and methods to insure the full range of life style options to all citizens.
C. Program gradual steps to adjust the economy of the County to the optimum range of population in "A" above.
D. Urge the transition of energy generation to other than fossil fuel sources.
H. Develop jointly with the Chamber of Commerce and Economic Development Agencies, methods of identifying, reporting and coping with <u>non-fiscal</u> costs of pollution.[6]

The Wayne County report is also notable for being what is probably the first local planning document to print the nongrowth economic analyses of Professor Herman E. Daly, a stationary-state economist from Louisana State University. The report devoted 25 pages to Daly's paper entitled "Toward a Stationary-State Economy," which was later included in a book.[7] It also contained numerous newspaper reprints covering nongrowth activities and environmental issues around the country.

FIRST CASUALTIES

Despite such encouraging efforts as those in Wayne and Orange Counties, planners working on some aspect of nongrowth in 1971 often had much more to worry about than getting national exposure and professional respect. Perhaps the first casualty, the Crispus Attucks of the nongrowth movement, was J. K. Smith, the director of the Tahoe Regional Planning Agency on the California-Nevada border. Smith, hired from a list of 725 applicants in 1970, developed a comprehensive plan for the fragile Lake Tahoe basin, using the McHarg approach and computer maps representing 59 types of environmental information on 22,000 ten-acre grids.

Smith's plan would have set the optimal population of the basin at 134,000. At the time the plan was released in May 1971, this figure was already being exceeded on busy weekends. Shortly thereafter, Smith's plan was rejected by the planning commission, and a local planner from nearby Placer County was hired to develop an alternate plan. He was later to succeed Smith as director. The local planner developed a plan that allowed for an optimal population size of nearly 280,000. This revised plan won a merit award from a local chapter of the American Institute of Planners (AIP).

Thus in 1971 and 1972, most planners advocating some form of nongrowth (usually some rather minor reduction in the rate of growth) were forced to adopt low profiles. I studied the origin of nongrowth movements in a number of communities and found the prevailing pattern to be one of strong citizen concern, usually precipitated by some traumatic new project or event, such as a regional shopping center, a new town, the overloading of a sewer system, or the introduction of a major new industry. The citizen pressure eventually reached the planner, who was then often forced into some kind of action—usually research on alternative futures. The Orange County, California, planners were among the few who really seem to have initiated a nongrowth effort and who have started at the policy level rather than undertaking a detailed program of research on basic data.

In those earlier days of nongrowth, and even today, planners could not help being impressed by the intensity of the debate that the subject can provoke. The size and weight of the "big guns" brought into action by the progrowth interests can also be intimidating. The opposition ranges from the hard hats of construction workers to the softer felt hats of seasoned attorneys. For example, when Boulder was debating a slow-growth charter amendment in 1971, a group of local businessmen known as "Forward Boulder" brought in Richard Babcock, a nationally known Chicago zoning and land use attorney and former president of ASPO's board of directors, to bolster their opposition. Babcock's general position on nongrowth is that it is usually a sham for exclusionary zoning, but he carries a lot of weight nationally and with ASPO. Few planners have dared to challenge him. (In fact, by the end of 1973 few if any of the prestigious planning and land use experts in the country had begun to explore the middle ground between nongrowth and social justice concerns.)

In Sacramento County, California, planners who advocated a rather modest urban limit line to contain sprawl were hit with a $40 million construction company lawsuit in April 1972. The company charged that members of the planning department had conspired to prevent the company from developing its property. In Montana, one mayor told me that if planners do not want to help put out all the brushfires associated with rapid growth they should get out of business or at least out of town.

Thus the planner's role in nongrowth is not an easy one. There is often mixed response to the concept from the local constituency. The opposition is usually capable of some hard shots. There has also been a general lack of support, recognition, and coordination of local efforts by the two major national planning organizations—ASPO and AIP, although ASPO has clearly been the more active of the two. The lack of support from above and below was especially significant in 1971 and 1972, although, as we illustrate in the next section, things began to change in 1973.

It is still not certain whether planners have backed off from nongrowth for internal or external reasons. One of the grand old men of the profession, Grady Clay, the editor of Landscape Architecture and the president of the ASPO Board of Directors, provided the following relevant comment:

> most of the planning-and-design professions have been so long hooked to growth, so long dependent upon continued physical urban growth to justify their own professional existence that it comes hard, looking a gift-horse in the mouth. Many younger planners/designers have no such problem: they look at growth and find it damnable or at least questionable.[8]

69

Clay reports that the ASPO board debated whether they dared
to accept "Planned Nongrowth" as the theme for the 1973 Los Angeles
convention. "They didn't," he noted; instead they opted for the theme
of "Planning for Varied Life Styles."

NONGROWTH BECOMES RESPECTABLE

In 1973, many planners began to learn that nongrowth, like
Watergate, would not go away just because they chose to ignore it.
As more and more reports, phone calls, and letters on local growth-
nongrowth debates flowed into ASPO's office in Chicago, a number of
staff members started to point with pride to the fact that we had done
work in this area. My planning advisory service report entitled Nongrowth as a Planning Alternative came out in September 1972 with
the cautious subtitle "A Preliminary Examination of an Emerging
Issue." In addition, the 1973 ASPO National Planning Conference,
held in Los Angeles in April, was the first national planning conference
to have formal nongrowth sessions on the program. The actual word
"nongrowth" was deemed to be too strong, however, so the sessions
were titled "Growth Controls." The morning session on April 9 was
subtitled "Cost Revenue Approaches to Growth," while the afternoon
session on the same day was subtitled "Legal Devices and Related
Issues." Between the two sessions, there was a luncheon that featured
speakers Robert Wood, the President of the University of Massachusetts, representing the U.S. Commission on Population Growth and
the American Future, and Mayor Peter Wilson of San Diego.
An interesting array of speakers enlightened and entertained
audiences of nearly 400 persons at both the morning and afternoon
assemblies. For the most part, the speakers were not the usual
"big names" or senior members of the planning profession. They
were, instead, people who had firsthand experience with local communities challenging growth. While there was one academic on each
panel, they had both worked closely with specific communities on
some aspect of nongrowth.
Later in 1973, a major, and far higher-priced, conference was
held in Chicago solely on the topic of growth—this time "managed
growth." The "National Conference on Managed Growth" was held
in September 1973 and was attended by over 400 people from over
40 states who paid as much as $275 each to attend the two-day affair.
This was not a planners' conference, although a number of planners
attended. It was put together by Urban Research Corporation, a
Chicago-based consulting firm.
The real thrust of the conference seemed to be toward attorneys
legitimizing or challenging various managed growth or nongrowth

concepts to concerned citizens and local political officials. Attendance
ranged from the 28-year-old mayor of Aspen, Colorado, to the middle-
aged member of a planning commission in a northern Florida community. There seemed to be a general desire to dispense with philosophical discussions and get on with some tried and true growth management techniques. Some attendees may have taken home the idea
of an urban limit line or moratorium ordinance, but the major significance of the conference was that so many paid so much to hear
so little. A sister conference on managed growth was held in New
York City in February 1974; compared with the first conference,
it was more oriented towards the development industry and less towards local officials.

PROSPECTS FOR EXPANDED PLANNING

Those in the business of shaping the futures of local communities are now prisoners of the realization that everything is relevant.
The "planning solution" is now seen as incorporating not only the
traditional physical issues, but as expanding ever outward to cover
fiscal, social, ecological, safety, seismic, archaeological, and a host
of other factors. Frustration mounts as the gap increases between
the kind of job that is acknowledged to be needed and the limited human
and data resources available to get the job done.

There are two possible solutions, both of which have been tried:

1. Creation of the renaissance man planner—a task that few
if any academic institutions are now carrying out, intend to carry
out, or are prepared to carry out. The problem of training such
planners is very much like that of training symphony orchestra
conductors. Such training depends on individual initiative—a motivated
person moving through a series of educational experiences, both
formal and work related, picking up pieces of the self-defined required gestalt.

2. Coordination between disciplines—in most cases, this is
more productive of confusion than of meaningful results. One con-
fronts the United Nations problem of the "babble of tongues" as the
botanist, sewer engineer, and attorney strive for a meaningful common denominator language.

Where will the knowledge and perspective required to implement plans and strategies in line with the "new mood" come from?
It is simpler to list at the outset the many places it will not come
from, at least not in the near future.

The Traditional Planning Schools

For various reasons, the nation's graduate planning schools have rendered themselves rather ineffective in producing persons equipped to take on the municipal planning challenges of the 1970s and 1980s. The most esteemed of the schools have only recently established their full citizenship in the academic community by developing Ph.D. programs. As part of the continuing preoccupation with status that has resulted, faculty choice leans towards Ph.D. requirements, bending the curriculum towards the theoretical and away from practical applications; Ph.D. candidates receive greatest faculty attention, since they are the "production measure" by which planning school faculty and administrators gauge their competitive success in the intramural academic environment; and non-Ph.D.s are often discouraged or prohibited from entering the faculty ranks, despite their expertise, experience, local exposure, or renaissance qualifications.

The result appears to be that the planning schools are producing a growing number of highly theoretically trained persons, equipped for and primarily interested in founding and staffing additional schools of planning. Each year the spiral seems to be taking the planning profession farther and farther away from concern for, and relevance to, the more immediate problems and issues of the day.

What retracking in the profession there has been in the past decade has more often come from student concern than from conscious incorporation of new issues by planning faculty, although some of it has come from faculty response to availability of federal funding flows that call for research on previously unexplored issues.

In the mid-1960s, for example, both patterns were operative and led to the incorporation of "social issues" into the planning curriculum. Students, sensitized to these issues, pressed for instruction in the social area. Not finding it in the traditional planning curriculum, they trooped, en masse, to the social work schools and sociology departments, in effect forcing designation of such courses as "acceptable electives." Over a period of years, starting with visiting lectureships from other departments, these concerns came to be more officially adopted into general planning curricula. Finally, planning faculty did not begin to become involved with social issues until federal funding became available, and readily obtainable, in that area. Legal issues related to planning became incorporated into the program in the same way. The common pattern was to begin with an occasional lecture to planning students by a law school faculty member, and eventually to move to joint appointments of faculty serving both schools.

72

In recent years, changes in planning education have continued to be forced by outside surges, though the issues have, of course, changed. There are beginning to be some exploratory federal funding flows from HUD, Council on Environmental Quality, National Science Foundation, and others. Some of this funding finds its way to academic institutions, and it is beginning to influence curriculum content. Student pressures for change are likewise evident. Entering students, often more conversant than faculty with the day-to-day issues in the communities from which they come, seek, where they can, to create informal seminars and formal class treatment of these issues. Their efforts have so far met with mixed success.

The Traditional Planning Offices

Most planning offices are characterized by what management consultants call "the problems of the aging institution." These problems are compounded by the problems associated with the traditional placement and generally accepted role of planning in the municipal structure. Many planning offices are now staffed, at top levels, by persons who reached their "level of competence" when the issues were far different from those confronted by today's and tomorrow's planning offices. The civil service status of these directors tends to ensure their lock-in and the preservation of their views of the world and ways of doing business, even in the face of growing citizen and decision maker demands for new, deeper, and more comprehensive approaches to the planning function. Over the years, planning departments have emphasized that their role is to provide frameworks for achieving long-range goals rather than to delve too deeply into the mechanics of influencing day-to-day decisions within a meaningful policy framework. In many ways, they have become captives of their previous statements and positions, and of the place they have accepted in the power structure. To press for a greater role, in light of the newly uncovered information on what planning can be or should be, would result in perhaps unbearable individual psychological wrenches for many, and political dislocations bearing great risk.

But staff planners will gradually shift, not so much because they feel it is right to do so, but because they are well-trained as responders. As citizens and decision makers continue to pressure for delivery of a different "planning product," that product will be delivered, as planners have always dutifully delivered it in the past. The heavy use of consultants and "outside help" in the first wave of nongrowth plans and strategies may be regarded as a testing of waters on the part of staff planners. New products are being demanded, but planners are not sure whether these demands should be regarded as

73

the fad of the moment or as something of more lasting import. Until the signals are more clear, it is generally regarded as safer to have such insights provided by shock troops, who can be sacrificed if findings are too politically unsettling. Only as acceptance of the new insights and approaches gradually builds will staff planners edge out of their conceptual boxes and begin to restructure their operations and their thinking to adjust to the new reality.

At the same time, we expect to see a small but significant and perhaps growing number of staff planners and planning directors fired, demoted, or encouraged to resign because they took a too active and challenging stance with regard to the nongrowth issue. The real tragedy will be that the few traumatic and publicized firings will result in a far greater number of cases of personal and professional cowardice.

The Municipal Management Profession

Two parallel developments bring those trained in public administration and municipal management more deeply into the nongrowth arena. First, municipal management training has been broadly expanding to the point where city managers are no longer worried just about the sweeping of streets or the correction of arithmetical errors on budget submissions. Training is sufficiently broad that graduates are now perhaps the only source of trained personnel who have any (even if not complete or detailed) understanding of all the decisions that influence growth or nongrowth. Second, as planning departments have failed to incorporate new needs and insights into traditional departmental activities, these activities—coordination of planning and capital budget, fiscal analysis, multidisciplinary review of PUD applications—have been lodged at other points in the municipal structure. These concerns are increasingly being handled by "departments of community development," which have responsibility for monitoring some of the more significant growth-inducing decisions. As planners, trapped by their historic role and their hesitancy to press for more power, have become relegated to the processing of applications and the preparation of harmless 20-year plans, the real action drifts toward the city manager or administrator's office, and deputy city managers often find themselves doing far more short-term and middle-range planning than the planning departments themselves.

74

WHERE DO WE GO FROM HERE ?

It could be argued that some growth, at the national level, is inevitable, at least until the year 2000 or 2010. Those who strongly emphasize the inevitability of growth, as the Rockefeller Task Force did in its report, The Use of Land: A Citizens' Policy Guide to Urban Growth,[9] have usually done a minimum of hard demographic research and tend to err on the high side in their projections. "There is bound to be some population growth," they reason, "and if the increase is not accommodated in one place, it will have to be accommodated in another. So let's plan for it everywhere by just doing a better job of planning, design, legal analysis, ordinance drafting, and so on."

It appears that we need a new, integrative profession to study growth and help people make informed decisions about whether they want more or less growth as a matter of public policy. This new profession need not supercede existing professions; it need only show potential and performance in dealing with growth in a comprehensive, yet pragmatically efficient manner. There are many questions that need to be addressed in connection with this recommendation. We deal with them briefly in the following paragraphs:[10]

1. We live in a complex, specialized society. How can we find "nongrowth professionals" who can do a better job on growth than the combined efforts of planners, attorneys, architects, economists, and so on?

Answer: Admittedly, it will be difficult. Perhaps the question holds the key to the answer. Maybe we have to develop a new breed of Renaissance persons who will be capable of looking at all aspects of the vital nongrowth questions simultaneously. They will have to be trained to consider energy, land use, social justice, environmental blackmail, birth control, death control, stationary state economics, and so on, and to make some sense of all these factors taken together. Wouldn't we all welcome people like this, given the present situation? Maybe they will appear only when the first flying saucer lands on earth. Maybe they are, even as we write, quietly training themselves, not waiting for academic institutions to create degree programs into which they can fit.

2. Maybe we could use a few more Renaissance men and women at the national or even world level, but so far most nongrowth activity in the United States has been at the local level. But do local communities need roving members of a new profession?

Answer: There is now substantial and growing nongrowth activity, most of it at the local level. But few people have been able to make much sense out of the varied and scattered local experiments with nongrowth. There is indeed a "new mood" in this country against unlimited population and economic growth, but we do not really know its full dimension, what caused it, how long it will endure, and what prices people are willing to pay to implement their new ideas.

We could use some professional expertise to interpret and assist the efforts of local communities (and eventually state and national governments), but most of our existing professions contain people educated under the old "growth is good" ethic. Also, the older and more powerful members of professions generally run things in most work situations, and they do not usually like radical changes. Who can think of a more radical change than nongrowth? We need a new profession to deal with nongrowth, starting perhaps at the local level and moving far and wide from that point.

3. Perhaps we do need a new profession to deal with the many and varied ripples moving out from the local nongrowth mood, but who is going to pay people to do such work?

Answer: Many planners have already found out that few people are willing to pay anyone to develop controversial or threatening ideas in public or on paper. The new nongrowth professionals will have to operate on a low-cost life style, first, in order to be sincere and, second, in order to minimize the corrupting effects of salaries, fees, and grants. For the immediate future, we suggest that those who want to work as nongrowth professionals also learn a trade or craft. Some nongrowthers could also become professional conference speakers, assuming that the nongrowth conference binge continues.

Those who want to specialize in nongrowth could also consider working undercover in a local planning department. For these people, we have the following advice: (a) Never rise higher than assistant director—keep the director around as a buffer, (b) Get the ear of a sympathetic assistant city attorney and sneak through some good ordinances, and (c) Always keep your bags packed.

4. How will the new nongrowth profession be able to avoid evolving towards the narrow-minded, self-serving stance taken by many of the existing professions?

Answer: All nongrowth professionals will have to sign a pledge to make their field obsolete in 5 to 10 years, either by achieving all their goals or else through mass resignations and public confessions of incompetence.

CONCLUSION

Nongrowth has important implications for our settlements, resources, personal lives, and institutions. Almost all of our professions originated in a world of plenty, a world of faith in growth and progress. A new world awaits our children, a world of scarcity of both resources and solutions. Thus, a new profession is needed to help us all slow things down. We are spending millions of dollars to help wipe out cancer. Why not spend a few hundred thousand to develop this new profession and help wipe out the cancer of rapid and wasteful growth?

NOTES

1. Earl Finkler, "New Orleans is a City Looking Over Its Shoulder," Planning (February-March 1971): 15.

2. Dennis L. Meadows et al., The Limits to Growth (New York: Universe Books, 1972).

3. William Lamont, "Memorandum." 3 June 1971. Paper forwarded by Boulder City Planning Department to American Society of Planning Officials. Duplicated.

4. Earl Finkler, Nongrowth as a Planning Alternative, Planning Advisory Service Report No. 283 (Chicago: American Society of Planning Officials, 1972).

5. Wayne County Planning Commission, Comprehensive Planning Process for Wayne County. II: Planning and the Environment (Detroit: May 1971), p. 4.

6. Ibid., p. 5.

7. Herman E. Daly, "Towards a Stationary-State Economy," in The Patient Earth, eds., John Harte and Robert Socolow (New York: Holt, Rinehart and Winston, 1971).

8. Grady Clay, "No Grow: Hot Property or a Hot Potato?" in Landscape Architecture (July 1973): 332.

9. William Reilly, ed. The Use of Land: A Citizens' Policy Guide to Urban Growth (New York: Thomas Y. Crowell, 1973).

10. The question-and-answer section of this chapter is a condensed version of Earl Finkler's article, "Nongrowth Professionals Needed to Help Slow Things Down," which appears in Landscape Architecture (April 1974).

6

STRATEGIES FOR
NONGROWTH PLANNING

Most communities are engaged in very intense battles for economic livelihood, political power, environmental quality, and access to opportunity. The issues being debated and fought about cover a broad range, and the weapons employed must have wide-ranging capabilities.

We do not attempt here to outline a foolproof program for stopping or controlling growth in every community. There is no such thing. The suggestions we put forward in this chapter are a potpourri of approaches that have been, and are being tried, in cities across the nation.

The nongrowth advocate's role must be, first and foremost, that of a diagnostician. Where are the leverage points in a community? Do they involve water supply, the sewer system, the general plan, attitude surveys, environmental impact statements, or perhaps recall of a council member or two? What works in Portland, Oregon, may be a foolish approach in Portland, Maine.

This overview of strategies, then, necessarily skips over some of the important fine points. Where possible, we have referred the reader to more detailed sources dealing with specific subject matter (as, for example, Bosselman, Callies, and Banta's The Taking Issue,[1] which deals with strategies for uses of police power controls) or with particular geographic areas (as, for example, the Stanford Environmental Law Society's excellent two-part "how to do it" series on growth control in California).[2]

AN OVERVIEW OF THE BATTLEFIELD

Responses to the nongrowth movement vary widely. Developers speak of the "foaming nongrowth mania." Those who firmly believe in such pessimistic predictions as those of the Club of Rome see participation in the nongrowth movement as the only way in which they can act with clear consciences, as a way to set in motion a series of forces that will stretch out the lifespan of earth for a few genera-tions (hopefully more). A fascinating, and perhaps frightening, aspect of the movement is that both those who are for it and those who are against it are acting in good faith, for the furtherance of their interests as they view them. There are few dilettantes or pure rabble-rousers or spoilers for a fight in the game. This is, for all concerned, a deadly serious business. While this chapter portrays builders and developers as the primary progrowth forces on the battlefield, it is also true that forces ranging from state highway departments to the Corps of Engineers to utility companies and others are often equally progrowth. We concentrate on builders and developers because they seem to have been the most visible progrowth advocates at the local community level to date.

The builder-developer fraternity builds its barricades behind the current rules of the game. (The Pacific Coast Builders Conference advertised that its 1974 annual meeting, the theme of which was "no-growth," would be "legally-oriented"—reviewing the significance of recent cases and rulings on nongrowth efforts.)

Local nongrowth advocates, following a tradition stemming from Holmes and Brandeis, point out the uses of the law as a vehicle for adapting slowly to public social and attitudinal concerns; gradually recasting itself, decision after decision, toward congruence with the mores and attitudinal climate of the day (though somewhat lagged, as a safety valve). Each small decision or local triumph is viewed as a small nudge on the tiller of the law, a continuing series of which will gradually redirect the ship to the appropriate course.

The "nongrowthers" may be viewed as lineal descendants of David Reisman and Robert Townsend in that they sense the propensity of bureaucratic institutions to continue to roll on their historic tracks, carrying past assumptions and world views as their baggage long after these perceptions, and the guidelines, programs, and actions that flow from them, have lost relevance to the realities of the world. Thus, nongrowthers realistically assume the role of the underdog, and the strategies appropriate to that role.

Those with significant financial resources at their disposal (and there are few nongrowthers among them) seek to influence change at those points in the decision process where dollars have meaning. Those without dollars, quite predictably, adopt the traditional tech-niques of visibility and publicity and use delaying tactics (realizing that to the developer, time is money—often significant amounts of money), sabotaging the structure through attempts to secure its break-down indirectly where efforts to confront it head-on are not productive.

So long as reasoned debate and resolution of the issues is not possible (and it appears that at the present time it generally is not), the antagonistic symbiosis between developer and nongrowther will escalate the battles of the day. Nongrowthers, without resources and without equal access to the decision-making process, will fight in the best traditions of insurgency and guerrilla warfare, assuming, perhaps realistically, that each battle may be their last. By doing so, however, the nongrowthers will discover that the laws of ecology operate in the home-building industry as well as in the natural setting. Only the strongest builder-developers will survive the nongrowth onslaught. Only those with the deepest pockets, the greatest ability to run the lengthening gauntlet of approvals, dedications, and contributions, will survive to fight as adversaries in the battles of the future. In winning one battle, the nongrowthers may unwittingly create adversaries even stronger than those they now face.

Similarly, and paradoxically, the smaller developers, who seek to preserve the system as it now exists, run the least chance of doing so by continuing on their current tack of blatant resistance. They may succeed in wiping out the nongrowthers, but in the process, they are likely to be wiped out themselves.

THE BUILDING INDUSTRY IN A
NONGROWTH WORLD

Before proceeding to outline some strategies, we describe, by way of introduction, the current and probable future attitudes of the homebuilding industry toward the nongrowth movement. As nongrowth and slow-growth techniques are refined and applied with greater effectiveness, builder and developer response is firming and opposition is strengthening. The proponents of controlled growth, though perhaps initially elated by the fact that the building industry was taking them seriously, have now come to realize that they are in for a long and intense battle. Many are beginning to question whether the initial nongrowth victories were somewhat Pyrrhic in nature, reflecting the fact that the building industry was caught momentarily off balance rather than defeated in head-to-head confrontation. After an initial period of confusion and disorientation, the industry has regrouped and begun to systematically direct its considerable resources against the nongrowth "enemy."

The current importance of the issue to the California building industry is illustrated by the fact that the theme of the 1974 Pacific Coast Builders Conference is "No Growth." Citing such nongrowth techniques as sewer connection denials and recall movements mounted against officials voting in favor of development, the president of the conference stated that "The wide range of day to day problems facing the home-building industry pales in contrast to the implications of the 'no growth' movement."

The nongrowth movement appears to be having two diametrically opposed effects on scale in the homebuilding industry. The general result seems to be the demise, or pending demise, of the middle-sized builder in many markets. As processing and public approval time and cost continue to increase, building firms that have sufficient financial strength to absorb these added costs fare better than smaller, less well capitalized firms. The Irvine Company, a major southern California community development organization, estimates that 10 percent or more of total project cost on most residential developments now goes for public approvals, processing, presentations, and so on. Some developers report as many as 35 to 40 different approvals required in connection with major residential projects. As complexities and uncertainties mount, lenders evaluate not only the feasibility of a project in traditional terms but also the developer's ability to weather the unexpected (but rather predictable) processing tangles that can add substantial time and cost to a development venture.

The nature of the regulatory system is also changing the development organization's definitions of "return on investment" and "profit." More firms are building to own, rather than building to sell on a quick in-and-out basis. As long-term investors in a given project, they are thus becoming more concerned with the qualitative aspects of projects, rather than merely being interested in the prospect of quick sales and cash flows. To quote one California Bay Area developer, "If we're going to be tied up with this thing for two or three years anyway, we might as well go the whole route, so that if we're stuck, we're stuck with something good."

Scale, however, has its limits, and at some undefined point economies turn to diseconomies. The large development organization, geared to production of 200 or more units each year, expands into new geographic areas as it finds that this production level cannot be generated within one market area. In southern California, the search for feasible projects has led builders from Los Angeles to Orange, to San Diego County, to the desert resort areas and on to Las Vegas, and on to Denver, Dallas, Phoenix, and other southwestern metropolitan areas. Increasingly, the site location specialist is greeted by the sound of doors slamming, since local firms, themselves attempting to produce to the limit of their organizational imperatives, have met whatever demand exists in metropolitan areas infected with the "foaming nongrowth mania."

The picture that emerges, then, is one in which the small local builder survives if he has knowledge of the unique specifics of his market, the large, well-capitalized development organization survives if it is not only well-capitalized but also sensitive to unique needs of local markets in which it operates, and the middle-sized builder is caught betwixt and between, required to move either up or down on the volume scale in order to survive.

A dilemma arises because much of the membership of local, regional, and national homebuilder associations consists of just such middle-sized builders, who are faced with the schizophrenic and frightening choice of altering their operations into one or another unfamiliar mode.

The political consequences are significant both within the industry and in the halls of local, state, and federal government. Homebuilders associations must represent the interests of their members. These interests, in the current marketplace, are often not at all clearly defined, and in most cases they lead to organizational attempts to bring back the development environment of the mid to late 1960s, where nearly everybody could survive, without giving too much thought to precise forward planning. In legislative halls, the pleas of the building industry are listened to attentively. In southern California, in such counties as Orange and San Diego, construction industry employment is moving to second place, and almost to first place, in terms of total county employment, as aerospace employment gradually declines. Whereas aerospace industry political support was distributed on a more nationwide basis, building industry political influence is closely and carefully distributed closer to the ground, and is a significant factor in elections—from local, city, and county supervisorial elections to state legislative and congressional campaigns.

The unemployed builder, however, occupies an anomalous position on the sympathy spectrum. Unemployed aerospace workers are clearly and generally recognized as victims of shifts in federal funding priorities. Retraining and reemployment strategies at the federal level are more quickly developed; in the case of aerospace workers, it may also have to do with the embarrassment of letting so much high-degree (master's level and Ph.D.) talent languish unproductively. Unemployed airline pilots and other airline employees can be readily identified as victims of the energy crisis; solutions to their problems may be forthcoming. Vietnam veterans can likewise clearly be shown to have done their part for the national cause; training and placement programs can be easily justified for them. But the builder has no such national flag in which to wrap himself, no clearly identifiable "devil" that can be identified as the source of his problems.

The homebuilding industry, throughout American history, has both benefited and suffered from the predominance of localized controls over its operations; it has not had to worry about the application of national standards, but it has not (until quite recently) been eligible for national funds.

If "nongrowth" catches on in communities throughout the nation as it appears to be doing at the national level, we are faced with the prospect of a vast segment of the U.S. homebuilding industry, in many major metropolitan markets, out of work, partly as the result of nongrowth (the visible demon), but more often as the result of other interacting forces, such as rising interest rates. And these particular unemployed are likely to languish without assistance, since they, unlike Lockheed, Amtrak, aerospace engineers, and Vietnam veterans, have no claim on either the federal conscience or the federal purse. However, many construction workers are extremely mobile and seem to find their way to new jobs in other areas, especially when local unemployment benefits maintain only about 20 percent of their normal income.

BUILDER STRATEGIES

Strategies used by builder-developer organizations to oppose growth limitation efforts are multiple and diverse. Some of the more prevalent are described in the following paragraphs.

The strategy of an increasing number of developer organizations appears to be to try to end-run the growing groundswell of antidevelopment sentiment by beating it to the state house and securing that bastion for as long as possible. Part of the force behind the "quiet revolution in land use controls"—the move upward from local to state regulation—may be explainable by the fact that developers are finding local governmental structures as unresponsive to their needs as are their environment-oriented or nongrowth-oriented tormentors. The local government system, which historically had been at the beck and call of developers, has now turned about on them and stands ready to do the bidding of the enemy. Organizations such as California's Western Developers Council place most of their lobbying effort at the state level, once they gain state legislative support for their positions they urge removal of land use control powers from local to higher levels of government. In many states, coalitions are being forged between the building industries, local jurisdictions anxious for property tax revenue, and labor interests, in the attempt to create state legislation receptive to development interests. (For example, a current California assembly bill would require an economic impact analysis of any proposed moratorium, regarding its effect on construction payrolls in the area in question.)

Some builder organizations have become active in furnishing technical assistance materials to their members. One California homebuilder association offered members a "No Growth Defense

Library," advertised as a weapon to help the developer "combat the no-growth mania," noting that

> Tight money comes and goes. . . . common are the ebb and
> flow of labor crises. . . . but NO GROWTH comes in like
> a swarm of locusts and stays to breed.

As noted in an earlier chapter, builder organizations are doing their part to contribute to the deepening pile of growth studies. Studies commissioned by the private sector are, not surprisingly, far more optimistic about the positive and beneficial impacts of growth than those done by or for public agencies. Developer studies generally document in graphic detail the alleged negative economic impact of construction industry unemployment. Such studies are heavily publicized in the local press and widely distributed. For example, copies of the recent "Ashley report," commissioned by the California Builders Council,[3] have been distributed free of charge to local planning directors and public officials. The hard-cover volume, resembling a Ph.D. thesis in both bulk and appearance, is a handsome addition to the professional library. It is available to civilians at $25 a copy.

Some developer organizations that have passed the point of purely emotional response concentrate all or part of their efforts on participation in local efforts to revise the development control system in order to reach a more equitable balance between private and public sector concerns. This "three yards and a cloud of dust" approach, while lacking in short-range publicity value, appears to hold promise as the stage of bargaining that will be reached by an increasing number of such organizations with the passage of time.

Increasingly, the building industry is taking its case to court. National and regional homebuilder organizations recognize quite well the legal momentum that can be generated out of one or a few favorable "test case" decisions. In 1973, the National Association of Home Builders reportedly assembled a litigation war chest of some $250,000 for use in selected test case situations. Resources of the fund have been used to develop the industry's case in response to local ordinances in communities such as Petaluma, California, and Pepper Pike, Ohio. (By comparison, the City of Petaluma circularized other California cities in the attempt to raise money to fund the legal defense of the city's growth control program. Contributions, in amounts down to $250, were received from at least thirty cities in the state.)

Recent Virginia litigation illustrates the range of issues that are brought into the argument against local efforts to implement growth control strategies. The situation involved attempts by the local government of Fairfax County, Virginia, and by state sewer and water agencies to limit the provision of sewer service to a potentially rapidly urbanizing segment of the Occaquan River basin. The following objections were raised in a class action complaint by four separate classes of plaintiffs. Class I consisted of nonresidents who sought to build on and occupy land that they then owned and that was zoned for development but not provided with adequate sewer service. They alleged that they were being denied their constitutional right to travel. Class II consisted of landowners whose land was zoned for development but who were unable to develop for profit because of lack of sewer facilities. They sued under the due process clause of the Constitution. Class III included owners of residences in the area who had bought with the expectation of eventual sewer service but who had not received sewer service, even though their taxes had increased in the interim holding period. They alleged that their property values had been inappropriately damaged. Class IV included owners of other properties in the sewered areas of the county who complained of the higher taxes they were forced to pay because of what they deemed the county's artificial (and unjustified) restriction of housing supply throughout the county at large.

In summary, it appears that the forces opposing nongrowth are well organized, well funded, and are working on multiple fronts. Strategies for implementation of nongrowth planning must be designed to counter a strong, determined, and often well-entrenched opposition.

STRATEGIES FOR ACHIEVING NONGROWTH

In discussing some possible strategies for achievement of nongrowth, the reader is again cautioned to look to the specifics of his or her own local situation and to develop detailed knowledge of the unique limits and opportunities that would make one technique more appropriate for that situation than another.

The description of strategies is intended to be illustrative rather than definitive. Those wishing to delve more deeply into the fine points are referred first to the numerous helpful references listed in the bibliography and then to their local attorneys and citizens' organizations.

It is difficult to classify any one technique as purely political, economic, or legal. Many embody elements of more than one of the above classifications—in fact, successful application may often require a multidisciplinary thrust. Since the effort involves the control of all forces that generate growth, the controls themselves are and must be multifaceted.

Attitude Change

A growing number of communities are recognizing the value of the "growth poll" or "community attitude survey" in altering local political attitudes toward the growth issue. Some observers, in fact, feel that such polls and surveys are "perhaps the most important implementation technique of all."[4]

Polls and surveys undertaken in local communities have varied in sophistication and meaningfulness. Many of the least effective are amateur efforts, often with questions so phrased as to lead to confirmation of the surveying organization's prejudgments on the growth issue. Even though these are often open to justified attack on methodological grounds, they have in many cases served to bring about changes in decision-maker attitudes. An increasing number of surveys, however, are professional efforts, utilizing professional public opinion survey firms or the resources of local university departments. (Use of university resources may explain, in part, the rapidity with which nongrowth sentiment has arisen in numerous college communities around the country. While, for reasons outlined elsewhere in this book, nongrowth sentiment is likely to be first evident and stronger in college communities, the availability of statistically oriented researchers ready to document the communities' sentiments may bring these changes of attitude more quickly to public view.) The Zero Population Growth organization has been most active in stimulating local polls and surveys of this kind and has prepared manuals of procedure for interested local communities.

City councils and other local government agencies generally have mixed emotions about participating in or lending of legitimacy to such survey efforts. This is particularly true when a local group with a known predisposition is the survey sponsor. Professionally conducted surveys by "objective outsiders" are more likely to receive public funding support and assistance. However, many elected officials prefer to rely on their own "radar" and sources of information from their constituents; they feel that surveys would reveal little that they were not already picking up through their own sources.

The resistance of local officials to participation in attitude surveys has weakened in some instances, most notably in situations (as in California) where elected officials have underestimated the strength of the environmental, ecological, or nongrowth sentiment and have been swept out of office by groundswells of electoral sentiment that had emerged for the first time at the polls. In other instances, elected officials realize that such a survey may, if results are sufficiently at variance with municipal policies and programs, be used as basis for a later referendum, initiative, or recall effort. Participation is viewed, in such cases, as an attempt of "co-option" or as insurance against the later use of survey results for political purposes.

Surveys are most valuable when they incorporate questions and answers that indicate the public's "willingness to pay" for achievement of a given objective or a specified quality of life. Without such realistic qualifiers, surveys are likely to show what one would expect them to show: existing residents strongly favor maintenance of things as they are—no more people, more open space, and maintenance and improvement of present facilities and services. It is only when respondents are forced to think about the prices—added tax dollars, in most cases—that must be paid to achieve these objectives, that they begin to think and respond in "trade-off terms" and to provide realistic feedback to local governments. Various municipal "gaming" and "simulation" exercises offer yet another means of introducing this "trade-off thinking" into municipal debates on the subject of growth. For example, planners with the Northeastern Illinois Planning Commission in Chicago have proposed using a very large hall with a map of the region covering the floor. Elected officials from the city and suburbs would be given houses and people units to allocate in their jurisdictions according to some overall regional population estimates prepared by the planners. These "group therapy" sessions are particularly valuable when they offer the opportunity for role-playing—when, for example, the builder is forced to see things from the ecologist's point of view, and vice versa. These efforts, while seldom directly effective in influencing the decision-making process, do have a longer-term value in loosening the preconceptions of all concerned and in improving the depth and quality of the debate.

Economic and Fiscal Analyses

Economic and fiscal analyses should be regarded, for reasons outlined in more detail in Chapter 4, primarily as vehicles for bringing about attitude change. They are more useful for this purpose than for actually implementing a nongrowth program. When done correctly, they provide much of the information that is needed to shape and tailor legal and budget implementation mechanisms and to counter the inevitable progrowth arguments.

While economic and fiscal information is increasingly used by both sides in court challenges to nongrowth programs, the availability of such information in the formative stages of program implementation can often serve to get the hard questions answered early on, or at least to focus the debate productively on specifics. When the tone of a local nongrowth debate is thus well set in the early innings, consensus can often emerge that reduces the likelihood of later court challenge.

Whether the issue involves a single residential project or a citywide general plan program, current political climates usually make implementation of nongrowth an exercise in compromise and negotiation. At least in the short term, advocates of nongrowth should be sufficiently well armed with economic information to be able to negotiate their way to meaningful partial victories when these appear to be the best of the available options.

The Hard-Line Strategies

The first wave of nongrowth sentiment resulted in a series of proposals for what might be regarded as "hard-line" strategies— definitive urban limited lines, population cap laws and housing unit cap laws to establish absolute limits on the numbers of persons or housing units that a given jurisdiction might accommodate, and city-wide open space zoning of remaining vacant land. Some of these pro-posals are described in more detail in Chapter 2.

Judicial and political response to most such solutions has generally been negative in recent months. While the law may be shift-ing towards an increasing recognition of public as well as private rights in land, the shift is gradual, perhaps more gradual than many nongrowth advocates had initially recognized. Planners, after back-ing off and licking their wounds, are returning with more cautious approaches that may end up achieving close to the same result, but with much more careful documentation in terms of performance criteria and more detailed laying of political foundations. Urban limit lines are now "floating urban limit lines," which may be bent and warped upon appropriate showings. The old general plan, which carried implicit and somewhat loosely defined population and housing "caps," is being revised, and the new plans gradually ratchet the hold-ing capacities downward.

Planning Powers and Related Controls

Planners are discovering that old wine may be the best wine— that the traditional planning techniques and mechanisms, if used more innovatively and more powerfully, may hold the answer. In other words, there appears to be no "magic" solution that traditional planners have been overlooking all these years. In fact, planners are now being asked, often for the first time, to make maximum use of the tools and techniques already available to them.

For many planners, these are exciting times. For others, the attempt to breathe life into existing mechanisms is a somewhat

sobering exercise. The recent California experience provides a good
example of the rapid shift in potential "planner power." Until 1973,
planning in the state proceeded on a "business as usual" basis. Plans
were prepared, duly adopted, and made available to reassure those
who were reassured by what they read in plans. Meanwhile, zoning
proceeded on its separate track, relatively unfettered by plan concepts.
Every few years, the plan was recolored to reflect the changes that
had taken place in the local land use pattern under the existing zoning.
Everybody was happy—there was planning for the planners and for
those who believed in planning, and zoning for those who believed in
development.

However, legislation that became effective in 1973 changed all
this by imposing a "consistency" requirement, which said, in effect,
that things would have to be in reality the way the planning textbooks
have always said they would and should be—zoning was to be regarded
as an implementing device for the concepts expressed in the general
plan. The separate tracks were merged. The plan now had meaning.
The state law now said that zoning had to be created so as to make the
plan concepts actually happen on the ground.

People in all quarters began to pay attention. Planners sharp-
ened their flow pens, knowing that what they were proposing might
really happen. Developer representatives began to appear at plan
hearings, aware that the plan had as much influence on their holdings
as the previous, separately negotiable zoning.

While we can not expect the transition from plan as symbol to
plan as reality to be this rapid in all jurisdictions, we submit that
the same process is going on, perhaps more subtly, in a large number
of states and cities. Plans are being tied to zoning and to capital
improvement budgets, and in the process they are becoming significant. Thus supplemented, plans have power, and the devices that
have always been theoretically available to control, shape, and direct
growth also gain power.

The Shift From Accommodative to Carrying-Capacity Planning

Most general plans and regulatory systems in the United States
are based on what might be called "accommodative planning." That
is, they incorporate projections of population and economic increase,
most of which are based on extrapolation of past trends, and plan the
use of land to best accommodate these trends in terms of added
housing units, added employment locations, and so on. As we gain
more insights about the impacts of economic and population growth
on various aspects of the environment (broadly defined here to include

ecological, physical, social, and fiscal environment), the entire structure of assumptions underlying municipal planning is beginning to
change to the point where these population and economic variables
are thought of as the dependent rather than the independent variables
in the system.

The shift is not, of course, occurring quickly or universally
throughout the nation. Individual efforts, coming from various sources
and dealing with various geographic areas, are gradually beginning
to incorporate the "carrying capacity" mentality into an increasing
proportion of planning activity.

Full implementation of the "carrying capacity" or "holding
capacity" approach will be difficult for a number of reasons. First,
accurate measurement of the many factors involved—air quality,
water quality, soil condition—is no simple task. Plans must incorporate a composite of all indicators, and face the problem of weighting
and of comparability between different forms of measurement.

Second, some observers feel that carrying capacity plans, at
their present stage of evolution, give too much weight to the more
easily identifiable physical factors and not enough to the social, fiscal,
psychological, and economic aspects of the urban equation, which are
more difficult to measure. Third, carrying capacity is not always a
static concept but can vary somewhat with technological developments
that improve "flushing capacity" or the ability of the environment to
absorb differing levels of impact from development. Some might contend that we have already flushed too much pollution into the environment, but others would counter that improved auto emission control
devices may, for example, increase the permissible number of cars
and road-miles in the system.

The unstable nature of the criteria themselves will lead to
hesitant adoption of the carrying capacity approach. For example,
reducing air pollution by adoption of strict auto emission controls
could significantly increase an area's holding capacity, thus requiring
revision of a broad range of land use controls and permitted densities.
In the meantime, long-term capital improvement investments might
have been made, based on the assumption of the lower "holding capacity." Local governments would be faced with a choice between costly
reinvestment and replanning, and settling for lower levels of development than could be satisfactorily accommodated. Given the traditional
propensity of most municipalities to "err on the high side," it seems
unlikely that a complete reversal of attitude, in the direction of sub-
optimizing, will be forthcoming.

Adoption of the approach might place some municipalities in
the embarrassing position of discovering that they had already developed beyond acceptable capacity. This direct confrontation of
nongrowth, or possibly even "managed decline," as public policy is
difficult to conceive even in these times of rapid attitude change.

Finally, measurements for most carrying-capacity indicators should be undertaken at a regional rather than a local level in order to reflect boundaries of air, water, or drainage basins. Regional government agencies, which have been historically underfunded, are likely to be slow to move into an active role in data provision.

Thus, it seems that the carrying-capacity approach, though of some theoretical validity, will not be adopted full scale as the basis for planning in any major region, at least in the short run. Rather, its influence will be felt on a random basis, as the capacities of local water supplies, sewers, and other facilities reach critical thresholds. Furthermore, these limitations will more often be imposed "from above"—in the form of EPA requirements, water quality control criteria, and similar criteria—than imposed on municipalities and regions by local decision makers.

The sum total of individual capacity limitations is beginning to impress itself on the public mind. Bond issues are scrutinized more carefully, local strategists are learning the value of gaining a majority of seats on previously ignored water districts. State and regional controls (such as California's Local Agency Formation Commissions) are being applied to the formerly free-wheeling special districts whose growth-inducing decisions and investments have often been more powerful than those of many cities. The planning process, then, does not flip quickly from the old way of doing business to the new. We are seeing a gradual shift and an increasing sensitivity, in many communities, to these significant factors in the growth equation.

Moratoriums

The moratorium, or total halt to development, is being employed in an increasing number of local jurisdictions. It can be imposed in the following ways:

1. by the local jurisdiction itself
2. by a service-providing agency external to the municipality (for example, an overloaded regional sewer service agency)
3. by the local electorate, in states where initiative powers permit
4. by state agencies applying override powers

At the present time, the moratorium generally does little more than buy time until something else happens—until a general plan revision is completed or a sewage treatment plant is constructed. Thus from the nongrowth advocate's point of view, the achievement of a moratorium should be regarded as far less important than effective use of time and resources to develop more permanent solutions while the moratorium remains in effect.

Downzoning

There is increasing evidence of willingness on the part of a number of jurisdictions to reduce permissible densities, or permissible use classifications, within their local zoning ordinances. The practice first became evident and popular in connection with the more obvious land use abuses—strip commercial zoning or long-unused high-density residential zoning. Even there, political battles surrounding the practice have been bloody, as owners with "technically vested rights" have fought against the reduction of the assumed development potential of their holdings.

Now, as the idea of rezoning has gained political backing, the practice is coming into increasing favor. Within existing incorporated cities it can take one of two forms, both equally beneficial to the cause of nongrowth. The first form is downzoning between classifications— for example, downzoning from a classification of R - 3 to R - 1. The second form is the shrinking of permissible densities within a classification. Instances abound of zoning classifications permitting densities of three to eight units to the acre, which generally result, for all practical purposes, in development of each applicant's parcel at or close to eight units to the acre.

The impact of such downzoning actions is less immediately visible than the impact of a moratorium or a timing approach, but even in the short run it can be equally beneficial in limiting growth pressures in a given area or in diverting growth pressures across the line into adjacent jurisdictions.

Batching of Development Applications

In most jurisdictions, requests for rezonings, and similar forms of special permission to develop in ways not covered in the normal planning framework, have been reviewed one at a time. This procedure has resulted, in many instances, in an oversolicitous regard for the circumstances of individual owners and an inability on the part of planning agencies and local decision makers to analyze adequately the cumulative impact of a series of seemingly harmless small approvals. The frustrations created by this approach have led to dissatisfaction with the environmental impact statement as a review and analysis mechanism. There is no question that the impacts generated by any one small subdivision are rather minimal in the

overall scheme of things; the problems arise when fifteen such subdivisions appear, one after the other, in the same valley. Present
review procedures generally do not provide an analytical framework
that permits identification of the combined, cumulative impacts of the
fifteen projects before any one is approved.

Some cities, such as Aspen, Colorado, have now instituted
"batching procedures" requiring that development requests be combined for hearing and review once or twice a year. Review under
such procedures permits planning staff to map and analyze the "hot
spots" of proposed activity and to make more meaningful recommendations to decision makers, on an area-by-area rather than project-by-
project basis.

Interim Zoning

Some describe this form of growth control as the "undeclared
moratorium." Numerous cities employ interim, holding, or "wait
and see" zones as growth staging, timing, and control devices, with
varying degrees of effectiveness. Examples include the 40-acre to
60-acre zoning categories employed by such California counties as
Napa, Santa Cruz, Marin, and Monterey. Since some alternative use
is permitted (technically at least, not all value is removed from the
land), this method seems to avoid taking problems in some states.
Zoning of this kind is a useful implementing device for plans that call
for incremental staging and phasing of development rather than for
the historically accepted leapfrog pattern.[5]

Timing and Phasing Strategies

A number of communities, such as those of Ramapo, New York,
and Petaluma, California, are preparing plans that call for gradual
staging of development. This strategy is a logical outgrowth of the
emerging tie between local planning and capital improvement budgeting.
Accordingly, it is most effective when the local jurisdiction itself has
control over infrastructure investment, less effective when responsibility for facility provision is fragmented among a number of independently operating special districts.

In some instances, as in Ramapo, for example, gradual staging
does not serve to reduce the total amount of development but rather
directs it more efficiently (in terms of public cost) over a longer
period of time than would have been the case had the development
industry had a greater say regarding the timing and location of individual projects. In other instances, such as the case of Petaluma,

the timing approach is tied to an absolute limit on numbers of permitted housing units—that is, timing is used as an implementing device
for a plan concept that has growth limitation as one of its central
principles. While a federal district court has recently found the
Petaluma approach to be overly restrictive, it is likely that other communities that can better document the public interest in slowed development will adopt timing and staging rationales, perhaps with implicit rather than explicit maximum limits.

Developer Exactions

The trend toward increasingly stiff exactions from the subdivider
or developer, through the use of subdivision regulation procedures,
has been gradually building over the past decade.[6] It has been fueled
by the triple forces of fiscal instability of local governments, dependent as they are on a slowly growing tax base in comparison to a
rapidly growing population base; growing demands for services on
the part of resident population; and increasing recognition of, and
ability to quantify, the externalities being sloughed onto the general
public by the subdivider. Exactions have increased—from parks and
open space to (in the case of a few jurisdictions) the provision of low
and moderate income housing, to (in a few but growing number of
cases) such social service facilities as day care centers.

Recognition of the fact that growth control objectives can be
achieved through combined use of the planning, zoning, and subdivision
regulation powers is leading to a gradual blending and integration of
these separate approval procedures into a combined "one stop" development ordinance through which all bargaining can be integrated.
Planned unit development ordinances were the first to combine these
forms of regulation; the American Law Institute's proposed model
Land Development Code recommends the procedure for general adoption.

In summary, it appears that in many jurisdictions significant
steps can be taken toward nongrowth merely by sharpening the planning tools that are currently available. This appears to be the
message of the recent publication The Taking Issue, in which Fred
Bosselman and David Callies administer a massive dose of encouragement to planning officials, city attorneys, and nongrowth advocates.

Bosselman and Callies point out that "taking" of private property is a legal term of art, defined differently in various jurisdictions, that is used in determining when public intrusion on private
property rights has been sufficiently great that compensation must
be paid to the individual owner. The case discussions in the book
show that balancing of interests is generally undertaken on a case-

by-case basis, with the equities of a given situation receiving greater consideration than general rules of law.

The recommendations and conclusions of the book seem to advise municipal planners and regulators not to get bogged down in legal technicalities but to recognize that the accumulation of specific court decisions will indicate the shift in public mood regarding what is and what is not appropriate public intervention into the private rights having to do with land development. The report almost seems to suggest that the ability of the public to regulate growth is as great as the ability of public agencies to soundly document and justify reasons for intervention.

Beyond the Local Planning Process

While there is much that can be done within the bounds of the local planning process, in numerous jurisdictions, help will have to be enlisted from other quarters as well. Other levers are available to the nongrowth advocate that should be used in support of, and supplementary to, an intensified local planning effort.

It is a recognized fact of planning life that local planning can range only as far as its elected overseers permit. Even if strong planning powers exist, they may lie dormant until and unless there is clear political support for their use. It thus appears appropriate to briefly list some of the leverage points that might be utilized to bring political sentiment and power into line with the nongrowth position.

1. The direct power of the vote should not be underestimated. While this approach may seem unattractive to those who prefer magic (or intricate technical or legal solutions) to hard work on mundane precinct-level matters, the fact is that sentiment built in this manner, through development of a mass public consciousness and voice, is definitely a valuable supplement to, and perhaps in some cases even a substitute for, the intricate plan or legal argument.

2. Pursuing this train of thought further—if the power of the vote is unsuccessful in the normal course of electoral events, the opportunity exists, in some areas, for concentrated pressure on certain officials, or against voting positions on critical issues, through the initiative, referendum, and recall procedures. While this shotgun approach may be a somewhat inefficient means for achieving progress in one jurisdiction, one should not overlook the effectiveness of the chain reaction that may reverberate out to other communities. A successful recall campaign in one city can often serve to strike fear into the hearts of councilpersons in adjacent cities, and to make them more receptive to changing attitudes.

3. As an additional end-run strategy, the possibility of gaining control over growth-inducing special districts should not be overlooked. If the water district is making the key growth-generating decisions, time and effort is better spent in that quarter than in attempts to influence a city council, whose role may be more of a symbolic and reactive nature.

Taking It Upstairs

There are a number of good reasons, many of which we have already mentioned, for having an increasing portion of the growth-influencing decisions made at higher levels of government—the regional or state level. One response to intractable local politics is to lobby for increased state oversight, even to the point of override, to ensure rational decision making on land use matters. As noted, developers have recognized the wisdom of this strategy, and for many nongrowth advocates and organizations, the challenge will be to beat the building industry and the progrowth forces to the state house. The search for higher-level solutions may be, in other words, a defensive rather than an offensive strategy.

Cities need not resort to the state house solely for the purpose of establishing higher-level decision-making authority. Cities may also be well advised to "go upstairs" for the purpose of getting more regulatory power transferred to the local level. Many cities exist at the present time as relatively hamstrung wards of their respective states. Before such jurisdictions can do any really effective planning for their local areas, it may be necessary for them to secure greater powers through state legislation in such areas as annexation, incorporation, extraterritorial planning and zoning powers, or revisions in distribution formulas for state-collected revenues.

Action Against Broader Economic Growth Forces

Local governments are recognizing that attempts to control the number of housing units or the number of people are attempts to deal with the growth problem very near "the end of the pipe." An increasing number of jurisdictions are tracing the chain backwards and trying to control the earlier, more significant growth-inducing decisions that inevitably result in more people and more housing units somewhere in the region. Regional agencies have recognized that without control over these more basic growth-inducing forces, they are limited to proposing strategies that address themselves more to questions of distribution than to questions of magnitude.

Cutting off "the growth fuel" has taken a number of diverse forms, some of them direct, some indirect. In Florida and Hawaii, public budgets for attraction of tourists are being either substantially cut or carefully examined and redirected. A number of cities in California and other states are similarly reducing, or exercising greater qualitative control over, budgets of industrial development and promotion agencies, such as chambers of commerce. The City of Los Angeles, for example, recently closed its New York industrial attraction office, after having concluded that the energy resources available to the city might be barely sufficient to service projected expansion of existing firms. A publicly funded redevelopment program in Utah is offering redevelopment land on a "scaled price" basis, with land prices lower for firms that agree to use local labor force in their operations and higher for firms that will import labor force. Less direct are the "stay away from here" publicity campaigns of such groups as Oregon's James G. Blaine Society (supported by public statements of the governor in the same vein) and the New Mexico Undevelopment Commission.

However, even the most aggressive of these efforts aimed at turning off the faucet of growth may be regarded as somewhat peripheral and symbolic in nature, though, to be sure, they are a short step in the right direction. In Orange County, California, for example, where both citizens and public agencies are developing numerous growth policies and plans, no effective attempts have been made to stem the flow of federal contracts to county firms or to influence federal location decisions, such as the recent decision to transfer perhaps as many as 3,000 federal employees to a million-square-foot building built by an aerospace contractor, but never occupied, in the south end of the county. So long as such growth-inducing decisions remain unaffected by local plans and policies, the local nongrowth effort will remain a distinctly uphill fight.

Achievement of nongrowth in any really effective sense of the term will require the simultaneous manipulation of a number of leverage points—local, regional, state, and federal; public and private; economic, legal, and political. A diverse and powerfully interacting set of forces and institutions combine to bring about growth. A similarly powerful set of countervailing forces and institutional mechanisms must be developed to bring growth under rational control. But the first, and perhaps, most important force in many instances is little more than a few community residents standing up and saying: "Enough growth is enough," or "Slow down," or may be just plain "Stop."

Guerilla Planning: How to Stop Growth in Ten Days

Most of this chapter and the book as a whole have dealt with the rather complex and longer-term issues involved in local nongrowth activity. Yet we know that many local people discover growth-related issues and consider appropriate responses in a simpler context and with a very short time frame. Since this book was written for the informed lay person as well as planners and other professionals, we are including a final fall-back strategy to be used when time is extremely short or when all else fails.

Given the pace of growth and development in many areas on the urban fringe and in relatively unspoiled areas, concerned citizens often learn about upcoming major changes—a new drive-in restaurant, a new subdivision, a new recreational complex—only a few weeks before some board or council hearing or decision-making meeting. Reactions to such news about minor, but potentially major, changes to the neighborhood, community, or environmental system tend to run from bitter resignation through apathy to the general feeling that something should be done to slow things down.

Here is a 10-day schedule for a community resident facing such potential growth and change:

1st day. Verify the facts. Call your neighbors. Better yet, call your city manager, planning director, or the reporter who covers local government. Don't let on that you are opposed at this point. Merely assume the objective tone of a citizen interested in the future of the community.

2nd day. Wait for the phone calls with delayed answers from a bureaucracy not prone to respond quickly to citizens concerned about the future of their community. Start collecting the telephone numbers of a few good attorneys, along with local citizens who know something about economics, land planning and zoning, the environment, architecture, and any other field pertinent to the matter at hand. A local university can be helpful in this regard, although often it is the students and not the professors who are eager to get involved in the community. Local high school teachers or faculty can also be helpful.

3rd day. By now you should have had some official reaction either verifying or denying the rumors. If not, call some relatively powerful political figure you know or can vote for or against and scream. When you have the basic facts and proposed timetable for zoning or subdivision approval, ask around about any planning or other published reports on the area or the proposed development.

Do not let agencies or offices mail these to you; you don't have time. Pick them up yourself. As you pick them up, say to the secretary or official, "Are you <u>sure</u> this is all you have on the subject?"

4th day. Now move into high gear. Disperse your information and concerns to a wide audience to try and pick up support. Maybe there is a local environmental or civic group that will want to take your cause as theirs. Be careful here; such groups often move in a different direction, or move too slowly to be helpful. If the proposed development seems both frightening and imminent, call an attorney. If his secretary says he is out playing golf with the head of the chamber of commerce, try another attorney.

5th day. Either defer to some leader who shares your opposition or elect yourself acting president of some ad hoc citizens group opposed to the project. This should be good for some media exposure. If not, go down to the local newspaper office on a slow day (Sundays or holidays are the best), present a short position paper, and offer yourself for an interview. Be careful not to wind up with the paper's real estate editor; real estate editors are usually caught up in the "building boom" mentality.

6th day. Keep an ear to the ground for reaction to your campaign. If there is none, don't worry. You have five days to go, and a certain amount of apathy on the part of potential opposition might be a blessing in disguise. Check your finances. This is the point where many well-meaning citizen efforts go broke. If your attorney is going to do anything other than send a few notes on his official letterhead, he should be able to summarize both his actions and his charges. Prepare an outline of any written submissions you are going to distribute at public meetings. If you haven't done so already, take an hour off to write down all you know and feel about the issue, in five pages or less, and circulate this to your fellows and to the media. A copy to the local planning office might also be appropriate.

179094

7th day. Rest. There is your health to consider. Besides, there will be many other battles you can fight and possibly win.

8th day. Last day to do any mailing. You should be in the phone call and personal meeting phase of your campaign. This might also be a good time to call or visit local politicians closest to you or to the issue. Try to get advance copies of agendas, planning reports, and so on that will be circulated at the hearing or meeting. Don't take no for an answer.

9th day. If all else has failed by this point, call your Congressman or Senator in Washington. You could also try one of Ralph Nader's groups in the same city. Contact the Center for Study of Responsive Law, P. O. Box 19367, Washington, D. C.; or the Citizen Action Group, 2000 P Street, N. W., Washington, D. C. 20036. Maybe there is some federal rule or requirement that would be helpful in delaying any local action.

A similar approach to the state is also possible, although this should probably be done earlier in the process. As a last resort, refine your most sensational findings of danger to public health, safety, or welfare and go down to your local radio, television, and newspaper offices to do your thing. As an example, you might try to delay a major new residential subdivision proposal by stating that the developer:

1. has done shoddy work elsewhere (try to find a real place where he has worked)
2. has been seen spending a lot of time and money in bars or resorts with local officials (watch out for the libel laws)
3. has failed to consider the historic importance of the area (reveal something relating to Indian artifacts or a possible Indian settlement)
4. has withheld adverse reports on the water table, soil conditions, erosion, flooding, etc.

This kind of last-minute strategy should be attempted only if you are desperate. Otherwise, consolidate your forces, check your handouts and position papers, and make sure that everyone (including your attorney) knows where and when the meeting is to be held.

10th day. This is it. Don't panic and do anything wild today. Make a few calls, arrange baby sitters and transportation and go to the meeting prepared to stay as long as it takes. Some officials try to delay controversial topics until the end of a meeting in the hope that citizens will get tired or bored and leave.

If there is an attempt to delay or defer consideration of the proposal and you feel really prepared, fight it and demand immediate consideration. On the other hand, if your major goal is to delay the proposal, argue for an even longer delay, but make sure you regroup your forces for all subsequent meetings.

NOTES

1. U.S. Council on Environmental Quality (Fred P. Bosselman and David Callies), The Taking Issue (Washington, D.C.: U.S. Government Printing Office, 1973).

100

2. Stanford Environmental Law Society, California Land Use Primer: A Legal Guide for Environmentalists (1972), and A Handbook for Controlling Local Growth (1973). Both available from the Society, Stanford Law School, Stanford, California.

3. Ashley Economic Services, Fiscal Impacts of Urban Growth (Sacramento: California Builders Council, 1974).

4. Remarks of Richard Rypinski, Chairman, Comprehensive Planning Organization of San Diego County, at Urban Research Corporation "Managed Growth" Conference, Chicago, September 1973.

5. For additional information on this technique, see Robert Freilich, "Interim Development Controls: Essential Tools for Implementing Flexible Planning and Zoning," Journal of Urban Law 49 (1971): 65.

6. See Richard Yearwood, Land Subdivision Regulation: Changing Principles and Practices (New York: Praeger, 1971).

I. General

Boulding, Kenneth E. "The Economics of the Coming Spaceship Earth." In Environmental Quality in a Growing Economy, edited by Henry Jarret. Baltimore: John Hopkins Press, 1966.

Cahn, Robert. "Where Do We Grow From Here?" A six-part series on land use in the Christian Science Monitor, May 21, 23, 25 and 30; and June 1 and 5, 1973.

Clawson, Marion. Suburban Land Conversion in the United States: an Economic and Governmental Process. Baltimore: Johns Hopkins Press, 1971.

Daly, Herman E., ed. Toward a Steady-State Economy. San Francisco: W. H. Freeman, 1973.

Density: Five Perspectives. Washington, D.C.: Urban Land Institute, 1972.

Finkler, Earl. Nongrowth as a Planning Alternative: A Preliminary Examination of an Emerging Issue. Chicago: American Society of Planning Officials, September 1972.

"Guiding Local Growth." Equilibrium 1, no. 1 (1973). (Issue devoted to local growth management) Palo Alto, Calif.: Zero Population Growth, Inc.

Hardin, Garrett. "The Tragedy of the Commons." In Toward a Steady-State Economy, edited by Herman E. Daly, pp. 133-148. San Francisco: W. H. Freeman, 1973; and Science, 13 December 1968, pp. 1243-48.

Hardin, Garrett. Exploring New Ethics for Survival. New York: Viking Press, 1972.

Kenney, Dr. Kenneth, et al. Urban Water Policy as an Input Into Urban Growth Policy. Knoxville, Tenn.: University of Tennessee, Water Resources Research Center, 1972.

"Managing Growth." Public Management, September 1973, p. 4. Report of the International City Managers' Association Committee on Growth and the Environment.

Meadows, D. H., et al. The Limits to Growth. New York: Universe Books, 1972.

Mishan, Ezra J. The Costs of Economic Growth. New York: Praeger, 1964.

Population and the American Future: Report of the Commission on Population Growth and the American Future. New York: New American Library, 1972.

Reilly, William, ed. The Use of Land: A Citizens' Policy Guide to Urban Growth. New York: Thomas Y. Crowell, 1973.

"The No-Growth Society." Daedalus 102, no. 4 (Fall 1973).

Ridker, Ronald K. "To Grow or Not to Grow: That's Not the Relevant Question." Science, 28 December 1973, p. 1315.

U.S. Council on Environmental Quality. Environmental and Economic Effects of Alternative Patterns of Land Development. Washington, D.C.: U.S. Government Printing Office, forthcoming 1974.

_____. (Fred P. Bosselman and David Callies.) The Quiet Revolution in Land Use Control. Washington, D.C.: U.S. Government Printing Office, December 1971.

_____. (Fred P. Bosselman, David Callies and John Banta.) The Taking Issue. Washington, D.C.: U.S. Government Printing Office, 1973.

_____. Economic and Environmental Effects of Leisure Home and Recreation Development. Washington, D.C.: U.S. Government Printing Office, forthcoming 1974.

U.S. Environmental Protection Agency. Alternative Futures and Environmental Quality. Washington, D.C.: U.S. Government Printing Office, 1973.

U.S. Environmental Protection Agency. Environmental Protection through Public and Private Development Controls. Washington, D.C.: U.S. Government Printing Office, 1973.

U.S. Executive Office of the President, Domestic Council. Report on National Growth. Washington, D.C.: U.S. Government Printing Office, 1972.

U.S., Senate, Committee on Interior and Insular Affairs. Land Use Policy and Planning Assistance Act. Report No. 93-197. Washington, D.C.: U.S. Government Printing Office, 1973.

Urban Land Institute. "Position Paper on National Land Use Legislation." Urban Land, December 1973.

Urban Research Corporation. Managed Growth. Chicago, 1973. (Compendium of articles on growth control from numerous local newspapers)

II. Cost-Revenue, Economic Aspects

Associated Home Builders of the Greater East Bay. Growth/Cost-Revenue Studies. Berkeley, 1972.

Connecticut Development Group, Residential Costs/Revenues Analysis Model. Hartford, Conn., 1973.

Crouch, R. L. and Weintraub, R. E. "Planned Unit Development: Cost-Benefit Analysis." Urban Land, June 1973, p. 4.

Gale, Dennis E. The Municipal Impact Evaluation System: Computer-Assisted Cost-Revenue Analysis of Urban Development. American Society of Planning Officials, Planning Advisory Service Report No. 294, September 1973.

Hirsch, Werner. Urban Economic Analysis. New York: McGraw-Hill, 1973.

Isard, Walter and Coughlin, Robert. Municipal Costs and Revenues Resulting from Community Growth. Wellesley, Mass.: Chandler-Davis, 1957.

Mace, Ruth L. and Wicker, Warren J. Do Single-Family Homes Pay Their Way? Research Monograph No. 15, Washington: Urban Land Institute, 1968.

Nature Conservancy. The Hidden Costs of Development. Arlington, Va., 1972.

San Diego Joint City-County Economic Analysis Task Force. The
Economics of Urbanization: Phase I Final Report. San Diego:
County of San Diego, Environmental Development Agency,
1973.

Stahl, David E. "Cost Repercussions of the No-Growth Movement."
Urban Land, December 1973, p. 17.

Sternlieb, George, et al. Housing Development and Municipal Costs.
New Brunswick, N.J.: Center for Urban Policy Research,
1973.

Thompson, Wilbur. "Economic Consequences of No-Growth."
AIA Journal, December 1973, p. 31.

III. City Costs Related to City Size

Baum, Paul. Issues in Optimal City Size. Special Report No. 3,
Housing, Real Estate, and Urban Land Studies Program,
University of California at Los Angeles, 1972.

Flax, Michael J. A Study in Comparative Urban Indicators: Conditions in 18 Large Metropolitan Areas. April 1972. Available
from the Publications Office, The Urban Institute, 2120 M
Street NW, Washington, D.C. 20037.

"Size Can Make a Difference: A Closer Look," ACIR Information
Bulletin No. 70-78. September 1970. Available from Advisory
Commission of Intergovernmental Relations, 726 Jackson
Place, N.W., Washington, D.C. 20575.

Veri, Albert R. "Density as an Environmental Issue." April 1972.
Available from Zero Population Growth, 4080 Fabian Way,
Palo Alto, California 94303.

IV. Nongrowth and the Poor

Agelasto, Michael. "No-Growth and the Poor: Equity Considerations
in Controlled Growth Policies." Planning Comment 9, nos. 1
and 2 (Spring 1973): 2-11. Available from Department of
City and Regional Planning, University of California, Berkeley,
California 94720.

Babcock, Richard F. and Bosselman, Fred P. Exclusionary Zoning:
Land Use Regulation and Housing in the 1970's New York:
Praeger, 1973.

105

Branfman, Eric J., Cohen, Benjamin I. and Trubek, David M. "Measuring the Invisible Wall: Land Use Controls and the Residential Patterns of the Poor." Yale Law Journal 82 (1973): 483.

Controlling Urban Growth—But for Whom? Available from the Potomac Institute, 1501 Eighteenth Street NW, Washington, D.C. 20036. March 1973.

Johnson, Willard R. "Should the Poor Buy No-Growth?" Daedalus 102, no. 4 (Fall 1973): 165.

Sagalyn, Marilyn and Sternlieb, George. Zoning and Housing Costs: the Impact of Land Use Controls on Housing Price. New Brunswick, N.J.: Center for Urban Policy Research, 1973.

Smith, James N., ed. Environmental Quality and Social Justice in Urban America. Washington, D.C.: Conservation Foundation, 1973.

Winslow, Mimi. "Growth Control and the Poor." Equilibrium 1, no. 1 (1973): 16

V. Carrying Capacity

Pacific Northwest River Basins Commission. Ecology and the Economy. Vancouver, Washington, 1972.

Pope, Carl. "Communities and Environments: Carrying Capacity." Equilibrium 1, no. 1 (January 1973): 12

State of Hawaii, Temporary Commission on Environmental Planning. A Plan for Hawaii's Environment. Honolulu, 1973.

U.S. Environmental Protection Agency. Alternative Futures and Environmental Quality. Washington, D.C.: U.S. Government Printing Office, 1973, pp. 102-30.

Von Wodtke, Mark, "The Carrying Capacity of the Los Angeles Basin." Cry California. Fall 1970.

Faulkner, Peter, and Horowitz, Jeffrey. Nuclear Services Corporation, Palo Alto, California. Unpublished analyses of San Francisco Bay Area.

VI. Legal Aspects

American Law Institute—American Bar Association (ALI-ABA).
Study Materials: Land Planning and Regulation of Development Seminar. November 1973. Compendium of papers and
articles.

Bosselman, Fred. "Can the Town of Ramapo Pass a Law to Bind
the Rights of the Whole World?" Florida State University
Law Review 1 (1973): 234.

Freilich, Robert. "Interim Development Controls: Essential Tools
for Implementing Flexible Planning and Zoning." Journal of
Urban Law 49 (1971): 65.

"The Legal Control of Population Growth and Distribution in a
Quality Environment: the Land Use Alternatives." Available
from Richard D. Lamm, University of Denver College of Law,
200 West 14th Ave., Denver, Colo. 80204.

"The Right to Travel: Another Constitutional Standard for Local
Land Use Regulation." University of Chicago Law Review 39
(1972): 612.

VII. Citizen Action

Community Action: How to Get it Successfully and Public Office
at the Local Level: How Does One Get Elected? Who Should
Try? Both of these booklets are available from the Center
for Information on America, Washington, Conn.

Population Poll Package. Samples of population polls and suggestions for conducting a poll in your community. Available from
Zero Population Growth, 4080 Fabian Way, Palo Alto, Calif.
94303.

Space for Survival: Blocking the Bulldozer in Urban America. A
Sierra Club Handbook. New York: Pocket Books, April 1971.

Stanford Environmental Law Society. California Land Use Primer:
A Legal Handbook for Environmentalists. Stanford, Calif.
November 1972.

Stanford Environmental Law Society. A Handbook for Controlling
Local Growth. Stanford, Calif., 1973.

VIII. Bibliographies

Agelasto, Michael. "No-Growth and the Poor: Equity Considerations in Controlled Growth Policies." Planning Comment 9, nos. 1 and 2 (Spring 1973): 10-11.

Council of Planning Librarians. Optimum City Size and Municipal Efficiency. Exchange Bibliography No. 169 (Monticello, Ill.).

Gale, Dennis. The Municipal Impact Evaluation System, Computer Assisted Cost/Revenue Analysis of Urban Development. Chicago: American Society of Planning Officials, pp. 31 ff. Selected, annotated, fiscal aspects.

Equilibrium 1, no. 1 (1973).

Equilibrium 1, no. 4 (1973): 44-45.

Finkler, Earl. Nongrowth: A Review of the Literature. Chicago: American Society of Planning Officials, March 1973.

Sternlieb, George, et al. Housing Development and Municipal Costs. New Brunswick, N.J.: Center for Urban Policy Research, 1973, p. 365. Municipal cost-revenue analysis, municipal expenditure analysis.

IX. Reporting Services

California Environmental Monitor. Environmental Research and Counsel, San Clemente, Calif. Monthly.

Urban Growth Letter. 854 National Press Bldg., Washington, D.C.

Growth Control Monitor. Housing and Development Reporter, Bureau of National Affairs, Washington, D.C.

Metropolitan Housing Program Memoranda, Potomac Institute, 1025 Connecticut Ave. NW, Washington, D.C.

Urban Research Corporation. Chicago, Ill.

X. State and Local Studies and Reports

Arizona

City of Tucson, Planning Division. Cost-Revenue Analysis by Land Use Zone. Tucson, Ariz., 1973.

California

General

Ashley Economic Services, Fiscal Impacts of Urban Growth. Sacramento: California Builders Council, 1974.

California, Senate, Local Government Committee, Subcommittee on Planning Law Revision. Hearing: Growth Control Legislation, October 15, 1973.

Heller, Alfred E. (ed.) The California Tomorrow Plan. San Francisco: California Tomorrow, 1971.

Fremont

Enders, Michael J. and Peterson, D. James. Financial and Market Analysis of the Proposed Development of a Portion of the Northern Plain Area of Fremont. CMR no. 185 (1972). Available from City Managers Office, City of Fremont Civic Center, Fremont, Calif. 94538.

Half Moon Bay

Paul, James T. "Do New Residential Developments Pay Their Own Way? A Case Study." In San Jose: Sprawling City. Appendix A, pp. 84-100. Available from Stanford Environmental Law Society, Stanford Law School, Stanford, Calif. 94305.

Kern County

Systems Management Associates. The Tejon Ranch Lake Project: An Evaluation of Its Impact on Kern County Taxpayers. Bakersfield, Calif., 1972.

Livermore

Gruen, Gruen and Associates. Impacts of Growth: An Analytical Framework and Fiscal Examples. San Francisco, 1972.

Los Angeles

Center for Futures Research. The Economic Impact of Declining Population Growth in Los Angeles County. Los Angeles: University of Southern California, 1973.

Orange County

Orange County Planning Department. People, Policy and Growth: A New Direction? Santa Ana, Calif., 1973.

Orange County Planning Department, Phase II Population Growth Study and Development Strategy Study. Santa Ana, Calif., 1972.

Palo Alto

Livingston and Blayney. Open Space vs. Development: Foothills Environmental Design Study. Palo Alto, Calif., 1971.

Real Estate Research Corporation. Economic Analysis of the Foothills Environmental Design Study. San Francisco, 1972.

Thorwaldson, Jay. "The Palo Alto Experience." Cry California 8, no. 2 (Spring 1973).

Petaluma
City of Petaluma. Environmental Design Plan. 1972

Pleasanton

Pleasanton General Plan Review: Alternate Growth Policies. Pleasanton, Calif., October 1972.

San Diego Region

Ashley Economic Services, Cost/Revenue Analysis of Housing Development in the City of San Diego. San Diego: SEED, Inc., 1972.

Comprehensive Planning Organization of the San Diego Region, Population Growth Policy Study: Sensitivity Analysis: Summary Report. San Diego, 1974.

Sierra Club, San Diego Chapter, Report on the Proposed Slow-Growth Initiative. San Diego, 1974.

San Francisco Bay Area

Association of Bay Area Governments: Formulation of Regional Growth Policy for the San Francisco Bay Region, Berkeley, 1972; Urban Growth Policy for the San Francisco Bay Region,

1972; Zoning and Growth in the San Francisco Bay Area, 1973.

San Jose

RAND Corporation. Alternate Growth Strategies for San Jose. (Reports of the RAND Urban Policy Analysis Project) Santa Monica, 1971-73.

Stanford Environmental Law Society. San Jose: Sprawling City, Stanford, Calif., 1971.

Santa Rosa

Livingston and Blayney. Santa Rosa Optimum Growth Report. Santa Rosa, 1973.

Thousand Oaks

Gruen, Gruen and Associates, Costs and Benefits of Alternative Open Space Policies. Thousand Oaks, Calif., 1973.

Colorado

Aurora

Aurora, Colorado Dept. of Planning and Community Development. Report on Population Growth in the City of Aurora: Rapid Growth—an Exploration into its Consequences. March 1973.

Boulder

Is Population Growth Good for Boulder Citizens? Eric Johnson. Available from Zero Population Growth, 4080 Fabian Way, Palo Alto, Calif., 1971.

Florida

General

Carter, Luther J. "Land Use Law (II): Florida is a Major Testing Ground." Science, 30 November, 1973, p. 902.

Myers, Phyllis. Slow Start in Paradise. Washington, D.C.: Conservation Foundation, 1974. (description of development of Florida land use legislation)

111

Boca Raton

Citizens for Reasonable Growth, Vote for Low Density, Boca
Raton, Fla., 1972.

Collier County

Density? An Analysis of Density As It Relates to Naples and
Coastal Collier County, Florida. Available from the Collier
County Conservancy, P.O. Box 2136, Naples, Fla., 33940.
November, 1972.

Manatee County

Manatee County Planning Dept. OPUG: A Growth Policy for
Manatee County, Florida. Bradenton, Fla., 1973.

Martin County

Peat, Marwick, Mitchell, and Co. Hutchinson Island Planning
Study: the Impact and Management of Growth. Stuart, Fla.,
1973.

Hawaii

Citizens for Hawaii. Maximillion Report. Honolulu, 1973.

"Report of the Temporary Commission on Population: State
of Hawaii." Available from Commission on Population
Stabilization, P.O. Box 2359, Honolulu, Hawaii 96804, January
1972.

"Some Questions and Answers on Act 187 or the State Zoning
Law" and "Facts about Act 205: Amendments to Act 187,
the State Zoning Law." Department of Planning and Economic
Development, 250 South King St., Honolulu, Hawaii 96813.

State of Hawaii, Dept. of Planning and Economic Development.
Central Oahu Planning Study. Honolulu, 1972.

State of Hawaii, Dept. of Planning and Economic Development.
Hawaii Growth Policies Plan: 1974-84. Honolulu, 1974.

State of Hawaii, Legislative Reference Bureau. In-Migration
As a Component of Hawaiian Population Growth. Honolulu,
1973.

Idaho

Ada Council of Governments. The Urban Form: An Analysis of the Social, Economic and Environmental Implications of Urban Expansion in the Boise Area. Boise, Idaho, 1973.

Illinois

Barton-Aschman Associates. The Barrington, Illinois Area: A Cost-Revenue Analysis of Land Use Alternatives. Chicago, 1970.

Stuart, Darwin G., and Treska, Robert B. "Who Pays for What?" Urban Land, March 1970, pp. 3-16.

Massachusetts

Old Colony Planning Council. Rapid Growth: A General Discussion of Problems and Solutions. Brockton, Massachusetts, 1973.

Michigan

City of Ann Arbor, Dept. of Planning. The Ann Arbor Growth Study. Ann Arbor, Mich., 1972.

Minnesota

Citizens League. Growth Without Sprawl. Minneapolis, 1973.

Metropolitan Council of the Twin Cities Area: Advantages and Disadvantages of Managing Metropolitan Growth, 1973; Costs of Providing Public Services to New Residential Development, 1973; Metropolitan Development Framework: Interim Policies, January 1974.

New Jersey

New Jersey County and Municipal Government Study Commission. Community Composition—Cost/Revenue. Trenton, N.J., 1973.

New Mexico

City of Santa Fe Planning Dept., Santa Fe Growth Impact Study. Santa Fe, N. Mex., 1973.

New York: Adirondack Area

Adirondack Park Act and Land Use Plan (ALI-ABA Study Materials compendium).

Ramapo

Chung, Hyung C. Controlling the Rate of Residential Growth: A Cost-Revenue Analysis for the Town of Ramapo, New York. Bridgeport, Conn.: University of Bridgeport, 1971.

Freilich, Robert. "Golden v. Town of Ramapo: Establishing a New Dimension in American Planning Law" Urban Lawyer 4 (Summer 1972): ix.

"Ramapo." Planning, July 1972, pp. 108-133. Published by American Society of Planning Officials, Chicago.

Oregon

Little, Charles E. The New Oregon Trail. Washington. D.C.: Conservation Foundation, 1974. (description of development of Oregon state land use legislation)

Mid-Willamette Valley Council of Governments, Salem, Oregon: Progress Reports: Proposed Urban Growth Policy, 1972-1973; Liveability and Urban Growth: Decisions and Directions Workshop, 1972; Costs of Growth for the Salem Area, 1972; Developmental Effects of an Urban Growth Boundary on the Salem Area, 1972; Combining Public Regulation and Public Compensation to Guide Urban Growth, 1972.

Vermont

Myers, Phyllis. So Goes Vermont. Washington, D.C.: Conservation Foundation, 1974, (description of development of Vermont state land use legislation)

Washington, D.C. Metropolitan Area

General

Gordon, Dr. Morton, et al. Optimum Growth: Consequences for the Year 2000 in Metropolitan Washington. Washington, D.C.: Metropolitan Washington Council of Governments, 1973.

Muller, Thomas. Fiscal Issues in Metropolitan Growth. Washington, D.C.: Metropolitan Washington Council of Governments, 1973.

Fairfax County, Va.

County of Fairfax, Division of Administrative Services. Five-Year County-Wide Development Program (3 volumes). Fairfax, Va., 1972.

Fairfax County, Citizens Committee on Fiscal Oversight. Toward a Sound Fiscal Program for a Healthy Community. Fairfax, Va., 1973.

Fairfax County, Task Force on Comprehensive Planning and Land Use Control. Proposal for Implementing an Improved Planning and Land Use Control System in Fairfax County. Fairfax, Va., 1973.

Population Reference Bureau. "Suburban Growth: A Case Study." Population Bulletin 28, no. 1 February, 1972.

Stansbury, Jeff. "Fairfax County: an Anatomy of Suburban Growth." Equilibrium 1, no. 1 (1973): 9.

Metro Metrics, Inc. Economics of Urban Growth: Costs and Benefits of Residential Construction. Washington, D.C., 1971.

Loudoun County, Va.

Vose, William O. Summary of the Economic Impact of the Levitt Planned Community in Loudoun County. Leesburg, Va.: Levitt Residential Communities, Inc., 1972.

Albemarle County, Va. (Charlottesville)

Muller, Thomas, and Grace Dawson. The Fiscal Impact of Residential and Commercial Development: A Case Study. Washington, D.C.: The Urban Institute, 1972.

Maryland

Impacts of New Town Zoning on Howard County, Maryland. Ellicott City, Md.: The Columbia Commission, 1971.

Tri-County Council for Southern Maryland. Impact of St. Charles Villages New Community. Walford, Md., 1972.

Doxiadis Urban Systems, Inc. Fiscal and Land Use Analysis of Prince George's County. Washington, D.C., 1970.

Prince George's County, Md. Proposed Staging Policy, 1973.

Wisconsin: Dane County (Madison)

More is Less: The Case Study of a City that May be Growing Too Big for its Citizens' Good. March 1973. Available from the Capital Community Citizens, 114 N. Carroll St., Madison, Wis. 53703.

Dane County Regional Planning Commission. Land Use Plan Alternatives for Dane County. Madison, Wis., 1972.

EARL L. FINKLER is a Principal Planner with the City of Tucson Planning Department in Tucson, Arizona. In 1974 he headed a ten-man city team preparing a comprehensive plan for the Tucson area. From 1970 to 1973 he was a Senior Research Associate with the American Society of Planning Officials in Chicago. While with ASPO, he authored such reports as Nongrowth as a Planning Alternative (1972) and Nongrowth: A Review of the Literature (1973). He has also worked as a local planner in the Arctic areas of Alaska and in Toronto.

Mr. Finkler has published articles on nongrowth in Landscape Architecture, Equilibrium magazine, the Chicago Tribune, and the Chicago Daily News. He received an M. A. in Urban Affairs from the University of Wisconsin—Milwaukee and a B. A. in Journalism from Marquette University.

DAVID L. PETERSON is a consulting planner based in Claremont, California. He has conducted numerous economic, housing, and growth policy analyses for public and private clients in the western United States. Before establishing his own practice in early 1973, he served, for four years, as vice-president of a major Los Angeles economic consulting firm.

Mr. Peterson received a B. A. degree in Social Psychology from Harvard College, an L. L. B. from Harvard Law School, and an M. A. in Urban Planning from the University of California at Berkeley. He currently teaches in the graduate planning program at the University of Southern California.

WILLIAM TONER is a Research Associate with the American Society of Planning Officials in Chicago. At ASPO he has coauthored Land Use Regulations for Sensitive Environmental Land Areas (1974) and has worked on projects dealing with land use controls in the urban fringe area. Previous to ASPO he coauthored People, Policy, and Growth: A New Direction? while working as a Growth Policy Analyst for the Orange County (Calif.) Planning Department. He is currently engaged in research dealing with local nongrowth economic strategies and with the preservation of prime agricultural land. Mr. Toner received a B. A. in Economics and an M. P. A. (Public Administration) from California State University at Fullerton.

AIR QUALITY MANAGEMENT AND LAND USE
PLANNING: Legal, Administrative, and
Methodological Perspectives   George Hagevik,
Daniel R. Mandelker,
and Richard K. Brail

ENVIRONMENTAL POLICY: Concepts and
International Implications
edited by Albert E. Utton
and Daniel H. Henning

ENVIRONMENTAL POLITICS edited by Stuart S. Nagel

EXCLUSIONARY ZONING: Lane Use Regulation
and Housing in the 1970s
Richard F. Babcock
and Fred P. Bosselman

INTEGRATION OF COASTAL ZONE SCIENCE
AND REGIONAL PLANNING   Lee Koppelman

MASS TRANSIT AND THE POLITICS OF
TECHNOLOGY: A Study of BART and the
San Francisco Bay Area   Stephen Zwerling

THE POLITICAL REALITIES OF URBAN
PLANNING   Don T. Allensworth